THE ALAMO

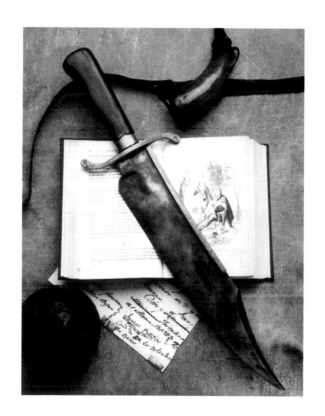

THE ALAMO

Frank Thompson

SALAMANDER

A Salamander Book

Published by Salamander Books Ltd.
8 Blenheim Court
Brewery Road
London N7 9NT

© Salamander Books Ltd., 2002

A member of Chrysalis Books plc

ISBN 1 84065 276 4

All correspondence concerning the content of this volume should be addressed to Salamander Books Ltd.

Credits

Project Manager: Ray Bonds
Designer: Heather Moore, Mitchell Print and Publishing Solutions
Colour reproduction: Anorax Imaging Ltd
Printed and bound in Taiwan

Author's Acknowledgements

This book is for Craig and Nina.

When any historian has the temerity to write about the Alamo, he does not act alone. He simply joins an army that has been maneuvering to occupy – or attack – the mission fort for nearly one hundred and seventy years. Whether the writer is a good soldier in this army or a mutinous malcontent, he can never labor under the delusion that he has worked independently of those who have gone before, or those who fight alongside him.

The bibliography at the end of this volume lists some – but by no means all – of the literature that has proved indispensable to me in my knowledge and understanding of the Alamo. I am in debt to every author represented there. Of these, there is a special place in my heart for the great Walter Lord, whose *A Time to Stand* remains the best, most compelling narrative history of the Alamo ever written. I was fortunate enough to meet Mr. Lord once – appropriately, on March 6, 1991, at New York's Alamo Restaurant – and I tried, inadequately, to convey to him then how much his work means to me. I am delighted to now have the chance to thank him in print for the enormous pleasure this and his other books have given me, and how crucial he was in setting me off on the road to the Alamo, so many years ago.

It would nearly fill this book if I were to list all the people who have assisted and befriended me over the years and who made a genuine contribution to this and everything I've written about the Alamo. Rather than slight any of them – and in the interest of saving precious paper – I'll simply list them in alphabetical order. My deepest gratitude goes to:

Dorothy Black, Mike and Nancy Boldt, Ray Bonds, Terry Borton, Quince Buteau, William R. Chemerka, Craig Covner, James Crisp, Angela Davis (Bob Bullock Texas State History Museum), William C. Davis, Donna and Mike Durrett, J. R.

The Author

Frank Thompson is an author, filmmaker, and film historian with a lifelong interest in the Alamo. Among his twenty books, prior to this, are two on the subject: *The Alamo: A Cultural History* (Taylor Publishing, 2001) and *Alamo Movies* (Republic of Texas Press, 1994). He has also written many articles on the subject in publications ranging from *Texas Monthly Magazine* to *The Philadelphia Inquirer*. As an Alamo authority, Thompson has appeared in the television documentaries "The Alamo" (the History Channel, 1996) and "History vs. Hollywood: The Alamo" (History Channel, 2001). As a producer, he prepared the current video releases of "Martyrs of the Alamo" (made in 1915), "With Davy Crockett at the Fall of the Alamo" (1926), "Heroes of the Alamo" (1937), and "The Alamo: Shrine of Texas Liberty" (1938). For the latter film, long believed lost, Thompson also wrote, produced and narrated a documentary, "The Alamo: Shrine of Texas Liberty ... Lost and Found" (2000). Frank Thompson lives in North Hollywood, California with his wife Claire.

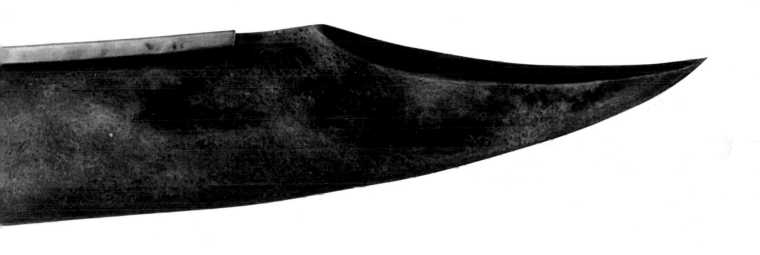

"Jack" Edmondson, Dan Gagliasso, John Andrew Gallagher, Mary Elizabeth Sue Goldman, Bill Groneman, Stephen Harrigan, Hank Harrison, Bela Herlong (Saluda County Historical Society), Jim and Barbara Higdon, Thomas W. Holland, Brian Huberman, Alan Huffines, Paul Andrew Hutton, Jack Jackson, Eric Jamborsky, John Jensen, Jack Judson, Ken Mahoney, Phil Martin, Joseph Musso, Sheryl O'Connell, Tony Pasqua, Ken Pruitt, Nina Rosenstand, Judith Sobre, Terry Todish, Tim Todish, Marc Wanamaker, Kevin R. Young and Gary Zaboly. -

Also, the staffs of the Ransom Center for the Humanities and the Barker Center for Western Studies, UT-Austin; the staff of the DRT Library at the Alamo, particularly Martha Utterback and the late Bernice Strong; the Saluda County (South Carolina) Historical Society; the Institute of Texan Cultures; and the Library of Congress.

Special thanks go to Stephen L. Hardin and Joseph Musso, both of whom very kindly read through my manuscript and gave me the benefit not only of their historical knowledge but of their keen editorial skill. Steve and Joe improved this book in countless ways – but whatever errors remain are mine.

And to Joan Headley, the Belle of the Alamo. Her fandangos are celebrated in song and story and no Alamo scholar can boast of the *compleat* San Antonio experience until he has passed at least one night in her fabled Crockett guest room.

Closer to home, I must thank Pete and Jake – and Molly in memoriam – for all the happiness and fleas they have brought into my life.

And eternal love and gratitude go to my beautiful Claire, whom posterity will someday recognize as history's greatest wife.

Frank Thompson,
Hollywood, California

CONTENTS

INTRODUCTION

In the afternoon of March 6, 1836, thick black smoke hung over the Alamo like an angry cloud. Hours earlier, before dawn, the place had been a nightmare of noise – gunfire, cannon blasts, shouts of rage, screams of agony. But now, the pall of silence that enveloped the ghastly scene was as palpable as the smoke, broken only by the pained murmurs of men going about their gruesome work or the stifled moans of the wounded. The sulfurous haze of battle had not quite dissipated; now it was augmented by the horrible black billows that poured skyward from three raging funeral pyres, consuming the corpses of more than two hundred men. The siege of the Alamo – and with it, the life of nearly every defender – was over. Now the remains of those defenders were consigned to the blaze, their ashes swirling up and away, as though desperately seeking to be free of this scene of terror, death, and defeat.

The horror of the Alamo would soon be nothing more than a memory. But the legend of the Alamo was in the process of being born,

flowing ever outward from the scene like the eddies that bore those ashes into the wind, spreading first to Texas, then to all points in the United States, then to every corner of the world.

When conquering General Antonio López de Santa Anna toured the blood-soaked ground in the hours after the final battle on that long-ago Sunday morning in March, he sneered that it had been only a skirmish, "a small affair." Of course, he was right. The siege lasted one day short of two weeks, was virtually bloodless on both sides and culminated in an assault that lasted barely an hour and left casualties that numbered in the hundreds, not the thousands. Compared to a *real* battle like Waterloo or D-Day, the Alamo seems like "a small affair" indeed. But its impact upon history has been formidable; it was a defeat that made victory possible. The bloodshed at the Alamo inspired and enraged Texans, Mexicans and Americans to take up arms against Santa Anna's dictatorship. Shouting "Remember the Alamo," Sam Houston's army defeated Santa Anna at San Jacinto barely six weeks later, on April 21, 1836, capturing the dictator himself and winning freedom for Texas.

This "small affair" had a powerful and literal impact upon the world around it. Because of it, Texas became a Republic and then one of the United States. But perhaps more important, the *meaning* of the Alamo has touched people of all nations. Millions, throughout history, have been inspired by the idea that a vastly outnumbered group of men so believed in the ideals for which they were fighting that they willingly laid down their lives for those ideals. The Alamo became a symbol of liberty, of sacrifice, of, as Commander William Barret Travis wrote, "everything dear to the American character." For Sam Houston's army, "Remember the Alamo" was a battle cry of vengeance. Today, the phrase means something else entirely. To "remember the Alamo" is to honor the sacrifice of the martyr, the determination of the patriot, the unshakeable belief in the sacred ideal of liberty and the necessity of defending that ideal, even unto death.

A dark cloud covered the Alamo on that day of death and defeat. A haze still envelops the Alamo today. It is no longer composed of the smoke of battle, or the billowing soot of the funeral pyres; instead, it is a cloud of myth that sometimes threatens to so thoroughly obscure the Alamo that the historical place and event seem in danger of getting lost in darkness; indeed, they become as but wisps of smoke themselves, impossible to hold onto or even see clearly. Never carefully documented at the time, many of the facts of the siege and

RIGHT: *A haunting portrait of the Alamo by moonlight by Jules Guerin. This painting originally appeared as an illustration in* The Ladies Home Journal, *April 1921. [Craig R. Covner Collection.]*

LEFT: *The mythic image of Davy Crockett standing before a lone Alamo church. In most people's minds, this single building was and is the Alamo. [Author Collection.]*

ABOVE: *This highly fanciful battle scene from the children's book* Exploring the New World *(Follett Publishing Co., Chicago, 1953) supports the popular view that the Alamo church constituted the entire fort in 1836. Here, the church is enormous, befitting its legendary stature. [Craig R. Covner Collection.]*

fall of the Alamo have become more and more remote over the decades; some have vanished into the ether, leaving some questions for which there will never be definite answers. The documentation that survives leaves enormous room for interpretation, allowing a great deal of leeway for even the most careful historian, offering contradictory points of view and uncertain testimonies. No wonder it is so easy still to get lost in that fog.

The bloody events at the Alamo can be seen only "through a glass darkly." Perhaps this is a crucial key to understanding why the battle has become such an important myth and why the beautiful, sad face of the only remaining building, the Alamo church, has become such an instantly recognized symbol, to all people everywhere. Because there is so much we don't know, we are given free rein to construct a truth that we find to be a comforting, inspiring model of behavior. In this sense, it is quite appropriate that the Alamo started life as a mission, for history's response to it has always been religious in nature. We can never know the precise details of the battle or the behavior and personalities of the people involved; we can only "believe" what our specific brand of faith allows us to. Like all religious subjects, the Alamo can be as divisive as it is inspiring. It has always been a

troubling reminder of racial differences, evoking a bitter past when Anglo and Hispanic have come to violence over issues of culture, politics and ethnicity. Because many of those issues have never been entirely resolved, the Alamo remains a controversial symbol. To many Hispanics, it represents not freedom and sacrifice, but the United States' relentless campaign of Manifest Destiny and a war that cost Mexico an enormous loss in lives and land.

But the Alamo has inspired other kinds of divisiveness, as well. Even those who are fascinated – even consumed – by the subject have found occasion to fight among themselves over matters of fact, interpretation, and meaning. Bitter enmities have erupted over the precise design of the Mexican shako or the exact nature of David Crockett's death; each warring faction fires volleys of research, hearsay, and accusations of bias into the ranks of the opposing army.

But just as the idea of the Alamo helped to give birth to the Republic – and later the State – of Texas, so can subsequent generations find in it new ideas and ideals of unity. The ancient mission continues to cast different kinds of spells over posterity; historians want to know exactly what happened there but others don't much care. The myth is all that is needed in order for the Alamo to continue to inspire and instruct. If that myth doesn't always gibe with the facts, then the facts are ignored or discarded completely. A character in John Ford's film *The Man Who Shot Liberty Valance* (1962) said, memorably, "When the legend becomes fact, print the legend." He might just as well have been speaking of the Alamo.

This book is, to the best of my ability, a factual account of the siege and fall of the Alamo, and of the events leading up to it, as well as the dramatic history of its aftermath. But it would be foolhardy to ignore the myths and legends of the Alamo. For one thing, some of them are so imbedded in our perceptions of the battle, that to omit them completely would be to cause some readers to assume that something of importance has been neglected. For another, no historical event exists only as something that *happened*; it is also – and perhaps just as important – how we interpret what we believe happened. It would be a disservice to the reader to report Alamo fiction as fact, but it would be wrongheaded to try and tell the story of the Alamo without addressing the meaning of the event and how that meaning continues to evolve. I hope to be an unbiased chronicler but I realize that this is impossible. My own

views of what happened at the Alamo, and what kind of people met on that bloody ground, must inevitably color how I read the research and present it to the reader. Everyone who writes about the subject faces the same struggle and each deals with it in his own way. John Myers Myers began his 1948 book *The Alamo* with an unabashed call to hero worship: "Those who doubt the greatness of men can leave this book alone or read it and recant."

I hope to take a far more even-handed approach than Myers, but doubtless my own point of view will constantly intrude upon the narrative. But I will at least make an attempt at fairness. The real siege and fall of the Alamo was far more complex than authors like Myers can admit, and the people involved – though some were undoubtedly "great" – were just humans, with all the good and bad qualities inherent in that condition; the same kind of humans who read about and evaluate their actions.

But no matter what meaning one draws from the bloody fracas at the Alamo, it is a fascinating, gripping story of resistance and resolve, of sacrifice and resurrection, of defeat and ultimate victory. It is a story that, in one sense, lasted thirteen days and, in another, perhaps greater, sense is not yet finished.

BELOW: *The 1950s and '60s saw a proliferation of children's stories, books, and toys related to the Alamo. This Sunday comic strip, "Little Orvy," originally ran in 1960. [Paul A. Hutton Collection.]*

THE PRELUDE

Stephen F. Austin felt betrayed. In 1833, Austin was Texas's leading colonist; indeed, he had done more to populate the vast territory with settlers from the United States than any other man. Now, he was sitting in a jail cell in Mexico City, without benefit of trial, with no idea when – or if – he would be paroled. Once so proud of his adopted role as a Mexican citizen that he preferred to be called "Esteban," Austin now dreamed dark dreams of revolt, of wresting the northern Mexican state of Texas from the hands of the country's dictator, Antonio López de Santa Anna.

Stephen's father, Moses Austin, was one of the authors of the Texas dream, having received permission from the Mexican government in 1820 to settle three hundred Anglo families in the territory. But Moses died before his plan could be carried out and he bequeathed his mission to Stephen.

It was a mission that met with Stephen's most heartfelt approval. "When I explored Texas in 1821," he wrote, "I was delighted and astonished at its natural beauties and many valuable resources."[1] It took two years, but Stephen finally brought in those settlers. The group was called the "Old Three Hundred," and they were only the beginning. In the following years, Austin settled fifteen hundred families in his promised land.

These settlers not only found a vast, fertile land of beauty and promise, but a government eager to make them feel at home. The Mexican government soon had laws in place that offered 4,428 acres of free land to any individual or family who agreed to settle there for a full decade. In fact, under the Mexican Constitution of 1824, the new arrivals wouldn't even have to pay taxes until that first decade had ended. To the thousands of colonists who accepted the offer, this seemed too good to be true.

They flocked to Texas from all over the United States – Tennessee, South Carolina, Georgia, Virginia, Illinois, Massachusetts, Pennsylvania, Louisiana and many other states – to build new futures in this wonderful, unsettled territory. The call went out beyond the United States, as well. Texas attracted settlers from nearly every country in Europe, such as France, Germany, England, Ireland, Scotland, and Denmark.

Most of these settlers agreed with Austin's appraisal of the vast Texas territory as a kind of paradise. The land was rich and fertile, the game was plentiful, the promise without end. One settler would call Texas "a heaven for men and dogs and a hell for women and oxen," but in those early days of settlement, its seemingly limitless potential made it seem almost magical.

ABOVE: *Stephen Fuller Austin as a young man.* [*Texas State Archives.*]

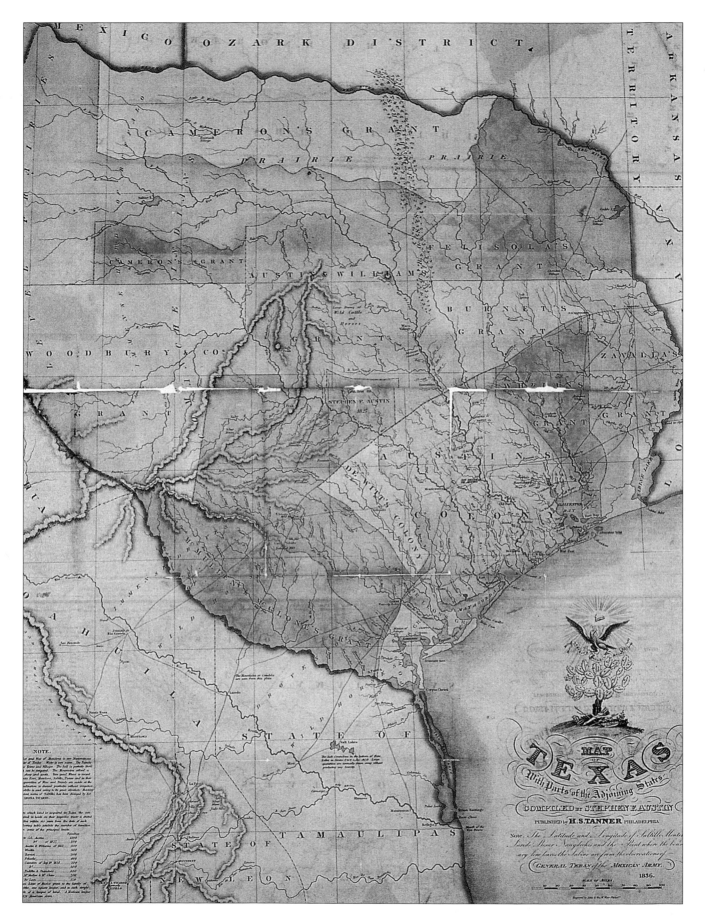

ABOVE: *An 1837 map of Texas, based on an earlier one by Stephen F. Austin. This map shows the major land grants as well as some unclaimed territory. [Library of Congress.]*

LEFT: *Austin reacts to news of an Indian attack on San Felipe by reaching for his rifle in this painting depicting the early days of the Texas colonies, in 1824. [Texas State Archives.]*

But the Mexican government's benevolence did not endure. By 1830, the borders began to close. Outsiders could no longer apply for Mexican land grants. Worse, Santa Anna abolished the Constitution of 1824 making Mexico, in essence, a dictatorship. He further angered colonists with the law that took away their exemption of duty taxes on all imported goods. Even those who had lived in Texas for more than a decade objected to paying taxes of any kind – so most of them just didn't bother.

To some in the Mexican government, the colonists' behavior seemed both inexplicable and rude. "For a long time, the ungrateful Texas colonists have made fun of the national laws of Mexico," wrote interim President Miguel Barragán on October 31, 1835. "Disregarding the fact that Mexico gave them a generous welcome and kept them close to our bosom; dispensing to them the same – and even more – benefits than to our own sons. Given the slightest opportunity, they returned to their aggression, throwing insults at our customs employees and even fighting the small detachments which protected them."[2]

What the Mexicans saw as benevolence, the colonists saw as tyranny. As more and more of their perceived "freedoms" began to disappear, the colonists became ever more resentful. Nearly seventy-five percent of all new citizens in Texas had come from the United States and many now began to advocate Texas's independence from Mexico – even if it took a revolution to do it. In 1831, when Mexico began enforcing its laws by stationing troops all over the territory, the stage for revolt was set.

Stephen Austin had long taken great pride in his ability to span the conflicting cultures of the Mexicans and their new Anglo-American colonists. In that spirit he urged the settlers – who, by now, had taken to calling themselves "Texians" not to act in a rash manner.

At the behest of the delegates of the Convention of 1833, Austin traveled to Mexico City with a list of reforms and a petition to repeal the law of April 6, 1830, which had forbidden the colonization in Texas by United States citizens. He was successful in his quest but, as he was returning home in December 1833, Austin was abruptly arrested "under suspicion of trying to incite insurrection in Texas, and taken back to Mexico City."[3]

Texas's greatest champion, and one of its most eloquent voices for compromise with the Mexican government, was left to rot in a cell, without trial or due process, for nearly two years.

The Stephen Austin who emerged from that prison 1835 was a changed man. No longer interested in maintaining friendly relations with Mexico, he was now in favor of Texas's independence. No longer an advocate of peace and tolerance, he openly urged his fellow colonists to prepare for war against Santa Anna. The changes in Austin were not limited to his philosophy but to his health. Seriously weakened by his imprisonment, he would be dead of pneumonia a year later – but he would live long enough to see Texas win its independence.

The first shots of the conflict were fired in October 1835 at the settlement of Gonzales, east of San Antonio. Under Lieutenant Francisco Castaneda, one hundred Mexican cavalry, of the Second Flying Company of El Alamo de Parras, had been dispatched to Gonzales to retrieve a six-pound cannon (that is, a cannon capable of firing a shell weighing six pounds) from the settlers. When they arrived, the Mexicans couldn't find the cannon. What they found instead was a determined group of about eighteen armed colonists under Colonel John Moore who called out defiantly that if the Mexicans wanted the cannon, they could "come and take it!" After an uneasy standoff for a couple of days, gunfire rang out at about dawn on October 2. The cannon in question was fired twice and the Mexican soldiers broke and ran. The little ruckus could barely be called a battle; it may have killed one Mexican soldier – probably wounded a few more. But it was immediately perceived as the Texas version of Lexington and Concord. These shots may not have been heard 'round the world, but the impact reverberated all the way to Mexico City.

FORTIFYING THE ALAMO

Coincidentally, the next day – October 3, 1835 – the Mexican National Congress awarded full control of the government to Santa Anna. The dictator had already sent General Martín Perfecto de Cos into Texas to occupy San Antonio de Béxar (or Béjar) – the largest town in Texas, and the territory's most important strategic point. Cos was instructed to put down all rebellion by the Texians. When he heard that the revolution had started at Gonzales, Cos moved his troops into Béxar, to occupy both the town and the old Mission San Antonio de Valero – popularly known as the Alamo – which stood east of town, just across the river. There, he joined the Colonel Domingo de Ugartecha, who commanded

(continued on page 21)

THE ALAMO MISSION

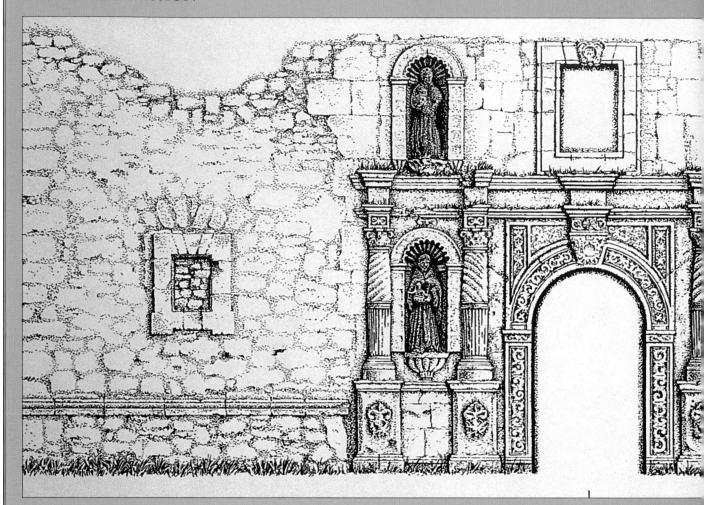

ABOVE: *Drawing of the church by Craig R. Covner shows the statues supposed to have been in place at the time of the battle. This drawing was a model sheet for the metal toy Alamo issued by Classic Toy Soldiers. [Courtesy Craig R. Covner.]*

Many visitors to the Alamo today take one look at the surviving building – the church – and comment on how small it is. They find it hard to believe that an epic battle which has lived in the world's imagination for nearly one hundred and seventy years could have been fought in such a tiny place.

In fact, the Alamo fell, in part, because it was too large. The surviving building is only one part of a large and unwieldy compound that started life as Mission San Antonio de Valero, the first of five San Antonio missions. As a mission, it offered plenty of room for dormitories, religious services, crops, animals, priests, and tenants. As a fort, it left much to be desired.

Construction on the Alamo church that survives today was begun in 1758, some forty years after Mission San Antonio de Valero was established. After several false starts at different locations around the area – the Alamo church kept collapsing and being rebuilt – the permanent mission was finally located east of San Antonio, just across the San Antonio River.

The little collection of homes called La Villita was several hundred yards to the south.

The compound covered an area of over three acres. The church, which was never completed, stood at the southeast corner of the trapezoid-shaped property. Built of enormous blocks of cream-colored limestone, the walls of the church were four feet thick.

The façade of the church was decorated with four icon niches, carved, spiraled columns framing the lower two. Two first floor windows were completed, as were all the ornate carvings around the door. Archeologist Jack D. Eaton created a conjectural view of what the church was apparently supposed to look like; it would have been a three-level building, with bell towers on each side. The upper icon niches were also to have been framed by columns, as was a single, centered niche on the third level. The entire structure was to be topped by a dome. The niches were to hold statues of St. Francis and St. Dominic on the first level, St. Claire and St. Margaret of Cortona on the second level, and Our Lady of

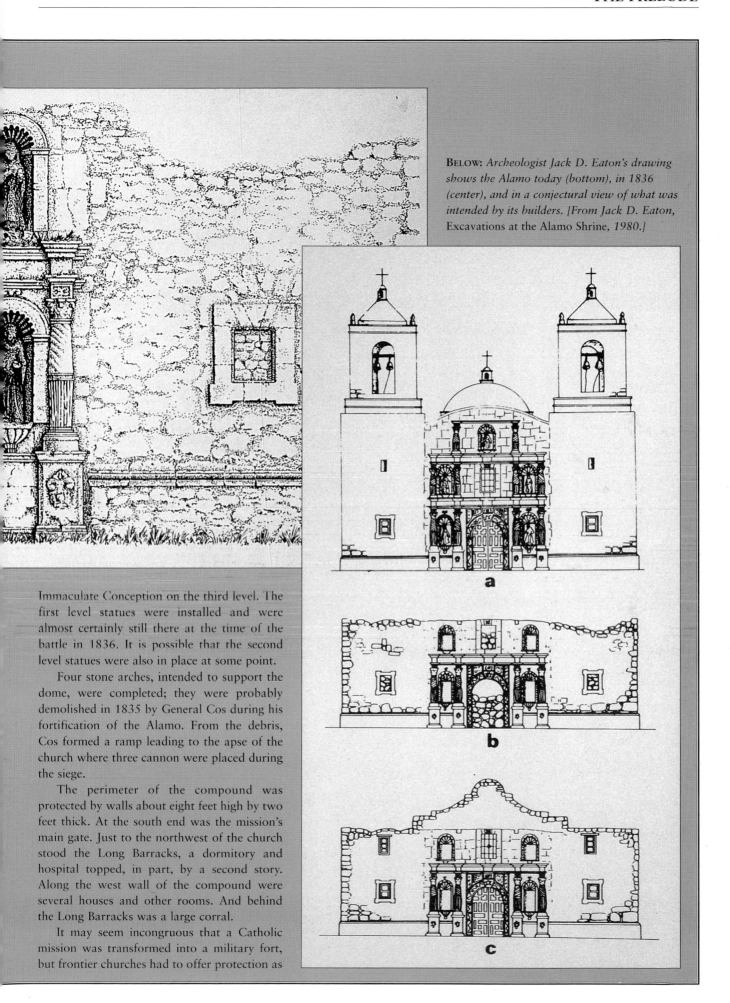

BELOW: *Archeologist Jack D. Eaton's drawing shows the Alamo today (bottom), in 1836 (center), and in a conjectural view of what was intended by its builders.* [From Jack D. Eaton, Excavations at the Alamo Shrine, 1980.]

Immaculate Conception on the third level. The first level statues were installed and were almost certainly still there at the time of the battle in 1836. It is possible that the second level statues were also in place at some point.

Four stone arches, intended to support the dome, were completed; they were probably demolished in 1835 by General Cos during his fortification of the Alamo. From the debris, Cos formed a ramp leading to the apse of the church where three cannon were placed during the siege.

The perimeter of the compound was protected by walls about eight feet high by two feet thick. At the south end was the mission's main gate. Just to the northwest of the church stood the Long Barracks, a dormitory and hospital topped, in part, by a second story. Along the west wall of the compound were several houses and other rooms. And behind the Long Barracks was a large corral.

It may seem incongruous that a Catholic mission was transformed into a military fort, but frontier churches had to offer protection as

well as spiritual solace. Of the five San Antonio missions, the Alamo was the strongest. But its size also made it unwieldy to defend – particularly by only a couple of hundred men.

But how did Mission San Antonio de Valero come to be called the Alamo? Some believe that it took its nickname from the double line of cottonwood trees planted along the Alameda nearby. The Spanish word for cottonwood is "alamo." But there is a more likely – and certainly more military – explanation. In about 1803, a Mexican cavalry company consisting of a hundred men was sent to occupy the Pueblo of San Antonio de Béxar. They came from a small town in Parras, Mexico, called San José y Santiago del Alamo. The cavalry unit called itself the Second Company of San Carlos de Alamo de Parras. Locally, they were known as the Alamo Company. And, eventually, the mission-turned-presidio where they lived was referred to simply as the Alamo. (For more information on the Second Company of San Carlos de Alamo de Parras and the Alamo in general, you may visit the Alamo de Parras website: www.Alamo-de-Parras.welkin.org.)

BELOW: *An 1836 map of the Alamo by José Juan Sánchez, sometimes known as Sánchez-Navarro. Although present at the battle of the Alamo, Sanchez actually drew this map after the battle of San Jacinto. [Barker Texas History Center, University of Texas-Austin.]*

about a thousand troops. The combined forces of Cos and Ugartecha, numbering approximately fourteen hundred men, set about strengthening the Alamo's walls and otherwise fortifying the place. Using the rubble inside the ruined church, they built a ramp that led up into the apse where three cannon could be placed. They shored up other sections of crumbling wall and built a palisade to close the long gap between the church and the Low Barracks/South Wall gate. From this position of strength, General Cos was ready to force the upstart Texians to surrender.

But it would be Cos who surrendered. Under the command of Stephen Austin, three-to-five hundred Texians lay siege to Béxar and the Alamo for the better part of a month, meeting – and defeating – Mexican troops in several engagements around the area. Led by Colonel James Bowie, with Captain James Fannin, the Texians scored a victory over the Mexican army south of Béxar, near Mission Purisima Concepción de Acuna. They captured a cannon, killing an estimated fifty Mexicans, and wounding perhaps sixty more. Only one of Bowie's men was killed, a

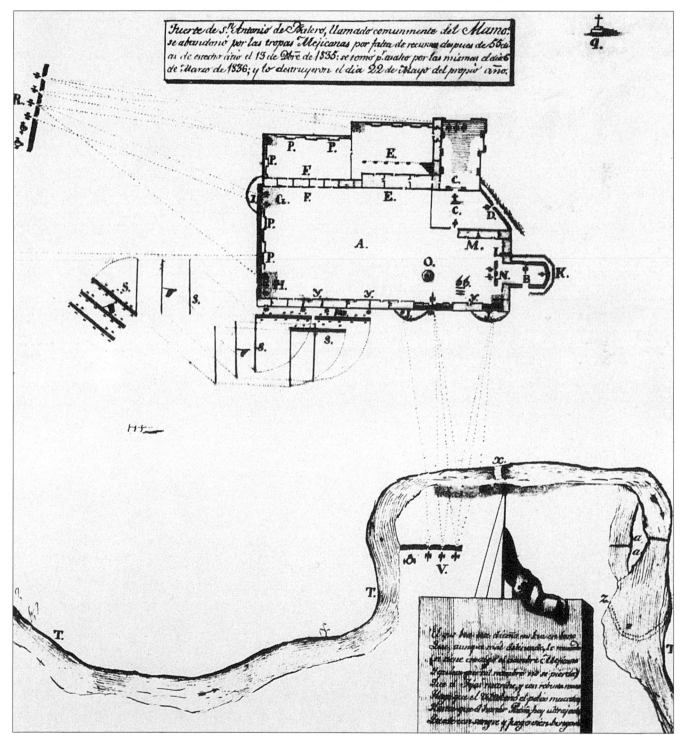

volunteer known as Big Dick Andrews; he was the first Texian fatality of the Revolution.

The Texians scored a somewhat less impressive victory about a month later when they attacked a Mexican mule pack train, which they believed to be carrying money and supplies into Béxar. When the battle was won and the Mexicans routed, the Texians, chagrinned, learned that the mules were carrying nothing more than fresh-cut grass to feed the garrison's horses. The episode became known – a bit sheepishly – as the "Grass Fight."

Meanwhile, the "Texas Consultation of the Chosen Delegates of All Texas" met at San Felipe to make a crucial decision – whether to force Santa Anna to restore the Mexican Constitution of 1824 or to simply take Texas away from him, establishing the territory as an independent Republic. Perhaps inevitably, for a group so predominantly composed of men from the United States, the lure of independence was simply too strong. On November 7, 1835, the delegates issued a manifesto, detailing their motives and intentions, among them "That Texas is no longer morally or civilly bound by the compact of union [with Mexico] ... That they do not acknowledge that the present authorities of the nominal Mexican republic

BELOW: *A contemporary engraving of Santa Anna. The artist has not particularly caught El Presidente's likeness, but he seems to have accurately captured some of the general's legendary hauteur. [American History Division, The New York Public Library.]*

have the right to govern within the limits of Texas … That they will not cease to carry on war against the said authorities whilst their troops are within the limits of Texas."

Back in Béxar, even though they had Cos surrounded, there was disagreement among the Texians on just what to do next. After laying siege for nearly a month, they were low on food, clothing, and supplies and morale was low. Volunteers continued to arrive, swelling the ranks to nearly a thousand men, but others left, arguing that their enlistment period was up. Texian General Edward Burleson was on the verge of withdrawing the army to Goliad, to hole up for the winter. Most of his officers agreed that withdrawing from Béxar seemed like a smart move.

But a frustrated fighter named Ben Milam did not agree. He and Burleson worked out a

compromise: Milam could call for volunteers to attack Cos. If enough of them were to step forward, then Burleson would keep his forces in Béxar for support.[4]

That was good enough for Milam. On December 4, he called out, "Boys, who will come with old Ben Milam into San Antonio?" It is said that he punctuated his call by drawing a line in the dirt with the butt of his rifle, encouraging those who would join him to step across the line. Two hundred and forty men, cheering their support, gathered at Milam's side. They began to prepare their attack, under the command of Milam and Colonel Frank Johnson.

Before dawn on December 5, 1835, the Texians began an attack on the Mexicans that would continue for four torturous days. The battle moved systematically from house to

ABOVE: *Henry Arthur McArdle's* Ben Milam Calling for Volunteers *(1901). [Craig R. Covner Collection.]*

23

house, men literally battering holes in the walls to move from one building to the next. The fighting was fierce but the Texians lost few men. Sadly, one of those killed in the assault was Ben Milam himself, shot by a sniper near the Veramendi Palace.

Once the town was in Texian hands, they moved on to the Alamo and easily took the fort as well. On December 9, Cos admitted defeat. He surrendered, but the Texians allowed him to keep his sword and go free, under the condition that neither he nor his officers would ever again "oppose the re-establishment of the Federal Constitution of 1824." Cos agreed and began leading his men south.

To Santa Anna, Cos's defeat was embarrassing and infuriating. The dictator believed that Cos should have easily suppressed the Texian rebellion and was outraged to learn that this ragtag aggregation of "pirates" had beaten his own professional army. In early December, he began marching toward San Antonio at the head of an army of several thousand men.

Meanwhile, the Texians continued the job that Cos started, that of fortifying the Alamo. General Sam Houston had appointed Colonel James C. Neill as the commander of the Texian forces at the Alamo. Neill understood the strategic position of San Antonio de Béxar and the importance of the Alamo as guardian of one of the major supply lines through Texas. But he also recognized its deficiencies as a fort and was keenly aware of how unprepared his own troops were for war.

Neill appointed Green B. Jameson, a former lawyer who had become the Alamo's engineer, to draw up plans for strengthening the three-acre compound. Under Jameson's direction, the men began to shore up the crumbling walls and try to turn the rambling mission into something that could reasonably be considered a fort. Jameson found the task to be a challenge. In a letter to Sam Houston on January 18, 1836, he wrote, "You can plainly see...that the Alamo was never built by

a military people for a fortress." Still, James admitted that it was "a strong place" and well armed with cannon. In case of attack, he promised, the Alamo defenders could "whip 10 to 1 with artillery."

But no matter how confident Jameson seemed, he realized that the Texians were in a potentially bad position. Only a month earlier, General Cos couldn't hold this sprawling old mission with nearly a thousand soldiers. And the Texians were now proposing doing it with fewer than 300 men.

Actually, by the time Jameson wrote to Houston, there were even fewer than that. Many of the Texians believed that the crucial place for fighting the revolution was farther south in Matamoros. On December 30, Colonel Frank Johnson and Colonel James Grant led two-thirds of the men out of the Alamo and began marching to Matamoros, taking with them most of the garrison's ammunition and supplies. That left Neill in

RIGHT: *A broadside issued by Governor Henry Smith during the siege of the Alamo. It may have raised the patriotic fervor of those who read it, but it raised few volunteers and proved to be of no help to the beleaguered Alamo defenders. [Texas State Library and Archives Commission.]*

LEFT: *The only portrait of William Barret Travis believed to have been drawn from life. [DeGolyer Library, Southern Methodist University, Dallas, Texas.]*

TEXAS

EXPECTS EVERY MAN TO DO HIS DUTY.

{ EXECUTIVE DEPARTMENT OF TEXAS.

FELLOW-CITIZENS OF TEXAS,

The enemy are upon us! A strong force surrounds the walls of San Antonio, and threaten that Garrison with the sword. Our country imperiously demands the service of every patriotic arm, and longer to continue in a state of *apathy* will be *criminal.* Citizens of Texas, descendants of Washington, awake! arouse yourselves!! The question is now to be decided, are we to continue as freemen, or bow beneath the rod of military despotism. Shall we, without a struggle, sacrifice our fortunes, our lives and our liberties, or shall we imitate the example of our forefathers, and hurl destruction upon the hands of our oppressors? The eyes of the world are upon us! All friends of liberty and of the rights of men, are anxious spectators of our conflict; or deeply enlisted in our cause. Shall we disappoint their hopes and expectations? No; let us at once fly to our arms, march to the battle field, meet the foe, and give renewed evidence to the world, that the arms of freemen, uplifted in defence of their rights and liberties, are irresistible. "Now is the day and now is the hour," that Texas expects every man to do his duty. Let us shew ourselves worthy to be free, *and we shall be free.* Our brethren of the United States have, with a generosity and a devotion to liberty, unparalleled in the annals of men, offered us every assistance. We have arms, ammunition, clothing and provisions; all we have to do, is to sustain ourselves for the present. Rest assured that succors will reach us,' and that the people of the United States will not permit the chains of slavery to be rivetted on us.

Fellow-Citizens, your garrison at San Antonio is surrounded by more than twenty times their numbers. Will you see them perish by the hands of a mercenary soldiery, without an effort for their relief? They cannot sustain the seige more than thirty days; for the sake of humanity, before that time give them succor. Citizens of the east, your brethren of the Brazos and Colorado, expect your assistance, afford it, and check the march of the enemy and suffer not your own land to become the seat of war; without your immediate aid we cannot sustain the war. Fellow-citizens, I call upon you as your executive officer to "turn out;" it is your country that demands your help. He who longer slumbers on the volcano, must be a madman. He who refuses to aid his country in this, her hour of peril and danger is a traitor. All persons able to bear arms in Texas are called on to rendezvous at the town of Gonzales, with the least possible delay armed and equipped for battle. *Our rights and liberties must be protected*; to the battle field march and save the country. An approving world smiles upon us, the God of battles is on our side, and victory awaits us.

Confidently believing that your energies will be sufficient for the occasion, and that your efforts will be ultimately successful. I subscribe myself your fellow-citizen,

HENRY SMITH,

Governor.

TEXAS
FOREVER!!

The usurper of the South has failed in his efforts to enslave the freemen of Texas.

The wives and daughters of Texas will be saved from the brutality of Mexican soldiers.

Now is the time to emigrate to the Garden of America.

A free passage, and all found, is offered at New Orleans to all applicants. Every settler receives a location of

EIGHT HUNDRED ACRES OF LAND.

On the 23d of February, a force of 1000 Mexicans came in sight of San Antonio, and on the 25th Gen. St. Anna arrived at that place with 2500 more men, and demanded a surrender of the fort held by 150 Texians, and on the refusal, he attempted to storm the fort, twice, with his whole force, but was repelled with the loss of 500 men, and the Americans lost none. Many of his troops, the liberals of Zacatecas, are brought on to Texas in irons and are urged forward with the promise of the women and plunder of Texas.

The Texian forces were marching to relieve St. Antonio, March the 2d. The Government of Texas is supplied with plenty of arms, ammunition, provisions, &c. &c.

charge of just about a hundred men – and they were dressed in rags and nearly starving.

On January 6, Neill wrote to Governor Smith:

"It may be appalling to you to learn and see herewith enclosed our alarming weakness... You, doubtless, have learned that we have no provision or clothing since Johnson and Grant left. If there has ever been a dollar here, I have no knowledge of it. The clothing sent here by the aid and patriotic exertions of the honorable council was taken from us by the arbitrary measure of Johnson and Grant, taken from men who endured all the hardships of winter, and who were not sufficiently clad for summer, many of them having but one blanket and one shirt... but if I have one hundred men, I will fight one thousand as long as I can and then not surrender."

But help was on the way. Sam Houston sent the famous knife fighter and adventurer James Bowie to take command of the Alamo. Once at the fort, Bowie agreed with Neill that the Alamo was a good place to mount their defense of Texas. On February 2, he wrote Governor Smith that, far from destroying the Alamo, "Colonel Neill and myself have come to the solemn resolve that we will rather die in these ditches than give it up to the enemy."

The next day, Lieutenant Colonel William Barret Travis arrived at the Alamo with about thirty men, and orders from Governor Smith to assist Bowie and Neill. The former South Carolinian was something of a firebrand, given to rather theatrical displays of valor. He was indisputably brave and a born leader who had taken a minor role in the siege of Béxar before going to San Felipe in November, 1835. Now, over a month later, Travis was not at all happy about being assigned to the Alamo. He wrote several plaintive letters to

Governor Smith, asking to be relieved of his command. Indeed, in one letter he offered to resign his commission. Smith, perhaps knowing that the hotheaded Travis had a tendency to blow off a certain amount of steam, never responded.

But as reluctant as he was to go to the Alamo, once there he recognized – as Bowie and Neill already had – the importance of the place. He wrote to Governor Smith, "It is more important to occupy this post than I imagined when I last saw you. It is the key to Texas."

In February 1836, the garrison of the Alamo received one exciting arrival and one disappointing departure within days of each other. The famous frontiersman and former United States Congressman David Crockett rode into Béxar with a few friends. He was known by all the Americans in the area and his presence among them must have struck them as a terribly good omen. Upon his arrival, like any good politician, Crockett gave a speech:

"I have come to aid you all that I can in your noble cause. I shall identify myself with your interests, and all the honor that I desire is that of defending as a high private, in common with my fellow citizens, the liberties of our common country." The arrival of Crockett and his "Tennessee Mounted Volunteers"[5] called for a high-spirited fandango on February 10.

The next morning, Colonel Neill left the fort for what he said would be twenty days' leave, claiming illness in his family. Neill passed on his command to Travis, who would lead the regulars. Bowie would remain in command of the volunteers who followed him. Travis, hoping to avoid a rift among the garrison, called for a vote – which Bowie easily won. In the end, they decided upon a joint command, and that they would make all major decisions as a team.

Soon enough, however, Travis would be in sole command of the Alamo. Bowie was ill, and quickly getting worse.

REFERENCES
1   Letter dated January 17, 1834.
2   Lamego, General Miguel A. Sanchez, *The Siege and Taking of the Alamo*. Santa Fe: The Press of the Territorian, 1968, p. 14.
3   Barker, Eugene C. "Austin, Stephen Fuller." The Handbook of Texas Online www.tsha.utexas.edu/handbook/online/articles/view/AA/fau14.html.
4   Hardin, Stephen L., *Texian Iliad*. Austin: University of Texas Press, 1996, pp. 77-78.
5   The Tennessee Mounted Volunteers were actually a group of about eighteen men under Captain William Harrison; "High Private" Crockett joined them in Nagogdoches and, because of his fame and charisma, assumed a kind of honorary command.

DEFENDERS
OF THE ALAMO

The Alamo garrison, in the popular imagination, consisted of coonskin cap-wearing frontiersman; bear hunters with long rifles and jackets with long strands of buckskin fringe; mountain men with no tolerance for civilized ways; hard-living, liberty-loving tough guys, ever on the lookout for a good fight or a stiff drink; simple men with a yen for freedom. In short, Americans – frontier-style.

Certainly some of the Alamo's defenders matched at least one of those descriptions, but reality is never quite as tidy as myth. In fact, the men of the Alamo represented a cross section of 1836 society. There were farmers and poets, storekeepers and teachers, musicians and sailors, doctors and lawyers – *lots* of lawyers. Most of the men had to qualify as hunters – gathering one's own food was still generally necessary for survival on the frontier — but they were, in the main, not wild men but bringers of civilization, men who wanted to create happy and safe communities with churches, schools and libraries, towns teeming with culture and prosperity.

BELOW: Battle of the Alamo *(1912) by Percy Moran. [Library of Congress.]*

Similarly, we have a tendency to think of the Alamo defenders as wearing outfits rather like that of the Davy Crockett of legend. But most of the Alamo's defenders were just ordinary citizens of 1836. And ordinary citizens of 1836, as a rule, did not wear fur hats. As historian Stephen L. Hardin has put it, "The vast majority of Texian revolutionaries would have resembled Oliver Twist far more than Natty Bumppo."[1] In most cases, this would mean tight, high-waisted trousers, vests, long tailed coats, and top hats. They often wore shirts with frills on the front and loosely wrapped ties. Beards and moustaches were not in fashion in 1836. Men wore their hair a little long, perhaps touching the tops of their ears and draping over their collars in back. Some wore long sideburns – which they would have called "whiskers" – that sometimes reached to the bottom of their ears and sometimes jutted all the way down to the jaw line. It was an era of formality, even on the frontier. Men typically owned few clothes but most were quite meticulous about keeping their limited wardrobe in good repair.

Almost all of them carried Kentucky-Pennsylvania long rifles, single-shot muzzleloaders that could hit a target up to two hundred yards away. The procedure to load and fire one of the rifles was complex and time-consuming but an accomplished marksman could fire and reload several times a minute under ideal circumstances. Men facing battle, however, would try to stockpile as many loaded rifles as possible.

There was room for variation of course. Perhaps some of the men carried single-shot flintlock pistols. Commander William Travis preferred the power of a shotgun. Probably every man in the garrison also carried a knife – butcher knives, mainly, but also stilettos, pocket knives or, of course, some variation of the popular "Bowie" knife.

(continued on page 44)

ABOVE: *A fanciful "portrait" of Jim Bowie – before an almost unrecognizable Alamo church – adorns this children's trading card from the 1940s. [Author Collection.]*

JAMES CLINTON NEILL

The original commander of the Alamo was certainly not the born leader that William Barret Travis was, but he does not quite deserve the obscurity into which history has placed him. General Houston thought enough of him to put him in charge of the crucial garrison at San Antonio, and James Bowie was so impressed with Neill's work at the Alamo that he made a philosophical about-face regarding the fort. Bowie arrived at the Alamo with, possibly, the aim of destroying it. But after being exposed to Neill's point of view for only a few days, he was ready to defend the Alamo to the death. Bowie wrote of Neill, "No other man in the army could have kept men at this post under the neglect they have experienced."

Neill was born in 1790 in North Carolina. He married and raised a family in Alabama, then moved them to Texas in 1831. When hostilities broke out, Neill joined the militia; in fact, it has been claimed that he actually fired the first shot of the revolution – at the "Come and Take It" fracas in Gonzales.

Neill left the Alamo due to an illness in the family, but he did not abandon the revolution for long. He worked tirelessly to raise money and reinforcements for the Alamo. On the very day the Alamo fell, Neill purchased medical supplies in Gonzales and set out for Béxar with about fifty men.

Having missed out on dying for Texas at the Alamo, Neill was present when Texas won her independence six weeks later. He commanded artillery, firing the Texian cannon, "the Twin Sisters," at San Jacinto. He was seriously wounded in the skirmishing preceding that battle. He died in 1845.

WILLIAM BARRET TRAVIS

William Barret Travis was far from the only lawyer in the Alamo garrison, but he may just have been the only one who was also a murderer – if legend is to be believed.

Born near Saluda, South Carolina, in 1809, Travis was the eldest of eleven children. As a child, he knew James Butler Bonham, who was born nearby and who would later die with him in the Alamo.

The Travises moved to Alabama in 1818 and William attended school there in Sparta and then Claiborne. He eventually began teaching in the latter school and married one of his students, Rosanna Cato, in 1828. He worked as an apprentice to the leading attorney in Claiborne and soon became a lawyer partner in the firm. He also published a newspaper, the *Claiborne Herald*.

Rosanna bore Travis a son, Charles Edward, on August 8, 1829. But before their second child was born a year later, William Barret Travis had left his family forever. It has been rumored that he suspected Rosanna of infidelity and was convinced that he was not the father of her second child. The rumors also suggest that he murdered Rosanna's lover, then fled for his life to Texas. There is no evidence to back up these rumors. It is true, however, that when Travis arrived in Texas he claimed at different times to be single and a widower.

Travis established a legal practice in Anahuac. He was himself, however, an illegal

Below: *The restored home of William Barret Travis in Perdue Hill, near Claiborne, Alabama. [Photograph by and courtesy of Joan Headley.]*

alien, having entered Texas after the edict by the Mexican government that forbade further immigration. He later moved to San Felipe de Austin and there became involved with the "War Party" – those colonists who were in favor of Texas independence.

He also became involved with Rebecca Cummings, and the two became engaged, planning to marry as soon as Travis's divorce from Rosanna was final. Ironically, although the divorce came through in the Autumn of 1835, Travis may have been too busy with the Texas Revolution to know it; there is no indication that he ever received the papers. He did, however, convince Rosanna to allow his son Charles to come to Texas to live with friends.

Travis had little military experience when he was sent to join Colonel Neill at the Alamo, yet he seems to have been a natural leader. Certainly, his letters from the Alamo are among the most eloquent and powerful of American documents. They also stand as the most thorough record of the siege from the Texian side. Crockett and Bowie may have been more famous, but twenty-six-year-old William Barret Travis was the moving force behind the Alamo garrison – its leader, its chronicler, its poet, its eulogist.

LEFT: *A panel from the mural in the Texas Hall of State in Dallas. It depicts that great mythic moment from the siege, Travis's drawing of the line. The mural,* Texas of History, *was created for the Centennial in 1936 by Yale University's Eugene Savage. [Dallas Historical Society.]*

35

JAMES BOWIE

James Bowie's fame today rests primarily on two factors – the imposing hunting knife which bore his name, and his death at the Alamo. Even by the time he arrived at the Alamo, Bowie was so renowned as a knife-fighter and adventurer that it would have been inconceivable to his fellow defenders – as it has been to history – that he would not turn out to be the fiercest fighter in the coming bloodbath. Alamo mythology has reluctantly conceded that he was confined to his bed during the battle of March 6 – but the tales always make sure that, before he dies, Bowie slays multiple enemy soldiers with his brace of pistols and, of course, his legendary blade.

Actually, the details of his death have been lost to history; there are no reliable eyewitness accounts that shed any light on his final moments. But, as with the death of Crockett, the details don't matter much – he died defending the Alamo, no doubt to the best of his ability.

James Bowie was born in Kentucky in 1796. His family moved to Louisiana a few years later. There, the enterprising Bowie worked any number of jobs, from farming and logging to buying and selling slaves – with the infamous pirate Jean Lafitte. The latter business made Bowie wealthy and he expanded his fortune through land speculation. He expanded his fame through acts of violence, heroism, and a quixotic quest. Even during his lifetime, most Americans knew of his legendary 1827 brawl, known as "the Sandbar Fight," in which Bowie, though seriously wounded himself, killed an opponent with a single thrust of a knife which eyewitnesses described as a "large butcher knife." Few reports of the duel omitted a description of the knife and soon men around the country were having "Bowie knives" made for themselves.

Then there was his quest for the San Saba silver mines in Texas. On one expedition, the brothers James and Rezin and nine companions were trapped for two days in the open countryside beyond the ruins of an old fort at San Saba, under siege by 164 Caddo Indians. It was an eerie prediction of the situation Bowie would later face in the Alamo, but this time Bowie and his men emerged triumphant. They claimed to have killed forty Indians and wounded thirty more.

James Bowie moved to Texas in 1830 and continued his land speculation, using methods that were not always strictly legal. He became a Mexican citizen and married wealthy Maria Ursula de Veramendi, the daughter of the governor of the state of Coahuila y Texas. She was also the goddaughter of Antonio López de Santa Anna.

After his wife died of cholera in 1833, Bowie devoted himself to the cause of Texas independence. He led the Texians to victory at Concepción and the "Grass Fight" and it was he who was chosen by Sam Houston to decide the fate of the fortifications in San Antonio and the Alamo itself. By the time the siege of the Alamo started, so had Bowie's illness – possibly typhoid fever, which may have developed into pneumonia. And so, ironically, one of the garrison's greatest and most famous fighters probably had little fight left in him by the time Santa Anna's soldiers entered the fort in the pre-dawn cold of March 6, 1836.

LEFT: *James Bowie in the only known oil painting of him done from life. Although unsigned, family tradition and the painting style indicate that it was painted by George Peter Alexander Healy ca. 1831-33. [Photograph of portrait by and courtesy of Joseph Musso.]*

RIGHT: *This original Bowie knife was formerly owned by U.S. Naval Officer Elisha Kent Kane and made by Henry Schively (1784-1863) of Philadelphia, Pennsylvania. Pictured with the knife is an original signed letter by Kane and an original carte-de-visite photo of Kane by Matthew Brady. The knife is lying across an original Mexican general's bicorne chapeau, stamped inside with British and Mexican proof marks and Queen Victoria's crown, indicating that it was made in England for Mexico during the years of Victoria's reign, 1837-1901. [Courtesy Joseph Musso.]*

DAVID CROCKETT

David Crockett was born in Tennessee on August 17, 1786. After a hardscrabble childhood – David was not much of a student – he married Polly Finley on August 14, 1806. They were soon the parents of two sons, William and John Wesley. Crockett worked his homestead with his family but proved more adept at hunting than farming. His prowess as a bear hunter was genuine and he would routinely supply his neighbors with all the bear meat they could use, simply because he was so good at tracking the creatures.

During the Creek Indian War, Crockett served briefly with the militia and, under

LEFT: *This portrait of David Crockett, ca. 1834, is attributed to artist John Neagle. [Courtesy Robert Weill and Joseph Musso.]*

BELOW: *A dignified David Crockett in an 1834 print based upon a lost painting by Samuel Osgood Crockett. [David Zucker Collection.]*

The members of the Alamo garrison became legends through their heroic deaths on March 6, 1836. But at least one member of their company was already a legend when he first walked through the Alamo's gate – the Honorable David Crockett from Tennessee. Having served two terms in the United States Congress helped to spread his fame, but most Americans preferred another Crockett – the bear hunting, Indian fighting trickster who described himself as "half horse, half alligator with a little touch of snapping turtle." They had read about this "Davy Crockett" in spurious autobiographies and the new "Crockett Almanacs," which were first published in 1835. And they had enjoyed the comic theatrical adventures of Colonel Nimrod Wildfire – clearly based upon Crockett – in James Kirk Pauldings' 1831 play "The Lion of the West."

In fact, after bridling at the Nimrod Wildfire connection at first, Crockett eventually came to embrace it. In 1833, Congressman Crockett attended a performance by James Hackett. When Hackett strode out on stage in the character of Colonel Nimrod Wildfire, resplendent in buckskin and fur hat, he paused for a moment to acknowledge Crockett. Smiling, Hackett bowed deeply. Crockett stood, and bowed back, to the delighted cheers of the audience. From then on, historical David and legendary Davy were officially intertwined.

Mr. Hackett as "Nimrod Wildfire."

From the original painting by A. Andrews in the possession of Thomas J. M.Kee Esq.

LEFT: *A portrait of actor James Hackett as Nimrod Wildfire from the popular play* The Lion of the West. *It has been suggested that this image became so intertwined with that of David Crockett that the Congressman began dressing in this fashion to please his public. Later Crockett "portraits" were based heavily on this illustration. [Courtesy Harvard Theater Collection.]*

General Andrew Jackson, fought in at least one fierce battle that turned into an Indian massacre. He was sickened by the carnage he witnessed but re-enlisted anyway. His wife Polly died in the summer of 1815, soon after giving birth to a daughter. Apparently feeling ill-equipped to handle three children on his own, Crockett soon married Elizabeth Patton, a widow with two children of her own.

Crockett's political career began in 1817 when he was elected Justice of the Peace. In 1921, he was elected to the State Legislature and then ran for a seat in Congress in 1825. He was defeated, but was successful when he tried again in 1827; he was reelected to a second term in 1829.

At first an ally of President Andrew Jackson, Crockett began to split with him philosophically, particularly on the issues of the rights of Indians to own their own land. Running for a third term, he was narrowly defeated by William Fitzgerald. But by now, Crockett was becoming a folk legend for reasons that had little to do with his political career. Indeed, his legendary status had a favorable impact on his political life and he managed to get elected to Congress again in 1833. However, in 1835, he was defeated again, this time by Adam Huntsman, a candidate with a wooden leg. Crockett made a memorable farewell address in Memphis: "Since you have chosen to elect a man with a timber toe to succeed me, you may all go to hell and I will go to Texas!"

To Crockett, Texas represented a new beginning. Still smarting from his political defeat, he liked the idea of going to a place filled with such promise and where his fame would automatically make him one of the prominent members of society. There is evidence that he even began to trade upon his legendary image. His youngest daughter Matilda later said that the last time she ever saw him, as he was boarding a steamship on the first leg of his trip to Texas, he was "dressed in his hunting shirt [and] wearing a coon skin cap," an outfit similar to that popularized by Nimrod Wildfire.

Once in Texas, he joined Captain William Harrison's company which some called the "Tennessee Mounted Volunteers." Although Crockett was just one of the boys, legend has always preferred to think of him as the leader of the band. Possibly, even the men of Harrison's company thought of him as one of their leaders; then, as now, fame virtually guaranteed prominence and authority. Indeed, history has always considered Crockett to be one of the commanders of the Alamo even though he himself admitted that he was nothing more than a "high private."

But fact and fancy always had a way of mixing themselves up in the life and legend of David Crockett. He came to Texas looking for a new beginning. What he found, just months before his fiftieth birthday, was immortality – and a myth that refuses to die.

JAMES BUTLER BONHAM

James Butler Bonham holds a place in the Alamo myth as one of its bravest defenders. Sent out by Travis as a courier, he is said to have replied, "I will report the results of my mission or die in the attempt!" Learning that help was not coming and that the fort was doomed, Bonham returned to the Alamo anyway, determined to keep his honor, even if it cost his life.

The details of this story have been amended over the years. Evidence now indicates that Bonham returned to the Alamo with a letter of hope, containing the news that reinforcements were on the way. He was not quite the messenger of doom that history has painted him. Yet, this new version of the events should not tarnish Bonham's bravery. The Alamo to which he returned was in a dangerous position, surrounded by the enemy, and there was always the possibility that the promised help would not arrive – as, indeed, it did not. Yet Bonham proved true to his word, reporting the results of his mission – and dying in (or at least as a result of) the attempt.

James Butler Bonham was born in 1807 and grew up only a few miles from young William Barret Travis near Saluda, South Carolina. Their families attended the same church; some historians suggest that they were even cousins. Novelists and filmmakers have turned them into boyhood chums but no evidence backs this up. They did, however, certainly know each other. Whether they remembered each other in the Alamo is a different question altogether.

Bonham became a lawyer in South Carolina and, apparently, quite a feisty one. He was once jailed for contempt when he threatened to tweak a judge's nose. In 1835, living in Alabama, he became interested in the cause of Texas independence, and helped to organize a company, the Mobile Greys, although he never served with them.

He arrived in Texas in November 1835. From San Felipe, on December 1, he wrote to Sam Houston, "Permit me, through you to volunteer my services in the present struggle of Texas without conditions. I shall receive nothing, either in the form of service pay, or lands, or rations." By December 20, Bonham had been commissioned a second lieutenant in the Texas cavalry. At the same time, he set up a legal office in Brazoria but Houston was more impressed with the military Bonham than the legal one. On January 11, 1836, Houston wrote of him, "His influence in the army is great – more so than some who 'would be generals'."

Bonham arrived in San Antonio de Béxar on January 19, 1836, possibly along with James Bowie's company. Once there, he made an unsuccessful bid to be one of the delegates to represent the Alamo garrison at the constitutional convention in Washington-on-the-Brazos.

Travis sent Bonham out with pleas for aid even before Santa Anna's army arrived on February 23. He returned to the Alamo on March 3, riding through Mexican lines from the direction of Powder House Hill, to the east of the fort.

It is believed that Bonham served on the cannon crew in the apse of the church but little is known about his defense in the Alamo or the manner of his death. But Bonham's place in the myth of the Alamo is secure; he stands just behind the "holy trinity" of Crockett, Bowie, and Travis, famed for his ride into the jaws of death, delivering the results of his mission, no matter what the cost.

BELOW: *Flat Grove, the birthplace of James Butler Bonham – and the only surviving birthplace of an Alamo hero – as it looked in 1900. [Courtesy Saluda County Historical Society.]*

Only a handful of the men had been born in Texas; these were *Tejanos* such as Toribio Losoya, Juan Abamillo, Damacio Jiminez, and Antonio Fuentes. The rest came from nearly every state in the Union and from several countries in Europe. A diverse sampling is as follows: Lemuel Crawford hailed from South Carolina; William Fontleroy, Kentucky; Samuel Evans, New York; James Dimpkins, England; Andrew Duvalt, Ireland; Charles Zanco, Denmark, William Linn, Massachusetts; William Thomas Malone, Georgia; William B. Harrison, Ohio. But of all the states, none contributed more men to the Alamo than Tennessee – nearly thirty in all hailed from the home of David Crockett.

Their professions were as diverse as their backgrounds. Captain Almeron Dickinson, who entered the Alamo with his wife Susannah and daughter Angelina, was a blacksmith by profession; Stephen Dennison, from Great Britain, was a glazier; Andrew Duvalt was a plasterer; Georgia's Manson Shied was a carpenter; and William Garnet was a Baptist preacher. Marcus Sewell of England made shoes; George Kimball of Pennsylvania made hats; Albert Martin of Rhode Island ran a store; Tennessee's Jesse

McCoy was a lawman – the Sheriff of Gonzales; Edward Mitchasson, of Virginia, was a doctor; Henry Warnell was a jockey; and North Carolina's Micajah Autry did it all – teacher, lawyer, poet, businessman.

Many of the Alamo defenders had personal histories with each other before entering the fort. Most famously, Commander William Barret Travis was a boyhood acquaintance of James Butler Bonham. The three Taylor brothers, Edward, James, and William, died together in the Alamo (Texas's Taylor County is named for them). John Harris perished there with his cousin, David Crockett. George Kimball had been in business with Almeron Dickinson. James George was married to the sister of fellow Alamo martyr William Dearduff, while Thomas Jackson was married to the sister of fellow defender George Washington Cottle.

They were as diverse a company as could be found in any area, anywhere. And their reasons for volunteering were many. A popular notion today is that the men of the Alamo were exactly what Santa Anna believed they were – pirates, land grabbers, slavers, all determined to use the resources of Texas for their own selfish ends. Being an inclusive

BELOW: *This heroic aggregation from the 1915 film* Martyrs of the Alamo *or* The Birth of Texas *still represents the public's image of the Alamo's defenders – stalwart, determined men in fur hats and buckskin jackets. [Author Collection.]*

LEFT: *A speculative portrait of William Barret Travis that probably bears little resemblance to the man. As usual, he is shown wearing a uniform. Actually, though Travis had ordered a uniform, there is no indication it reached him before his death. [Author Collection.]*

cross-section of society, no doubt the Alamo garrison did indeed contain at least a few men with just those attributes. But most seem to have been inspired by the vast promise of Texas and naturally drawn to a fight for liberty.

William Dewees wrote, "We're here all united together, bound together by an indissoluble tie." Daniel Cloud agreed: "The cause of philanthropy, of humanity, of liberty and human happiness throughout the world calls loudly on every man who can, to aid Texas... if we succeed, a fertile region and a grateful people will be for us our home and secure to us our reward. If we fail, death in defense of so just and so good a cause need not excite a shudder or a tear." Micajah Autry felt the same way: "I go whole Hog in the cause of Texas. I expect to help them gain their independence and also to form their civil government, for it is worth risking many lives for."

Some came to Texas to answer liberty's call, others to take advantage of the free land and its attendant possibility of wealth and power. Others ran away to Texas in much the same spirit as European men were running away to join the newly formed French Foreign Legion – to start again, to cut unpleasant family ties, to escape the law, to forget. David Crockett saw Texas as a new beginning after a galling defeat in Congress. William Barret Travis was fleeing a bad marriage and crushing debts. The newly widowed John Forsyth hoped that Texas would ease his grief. The rambunctious Henry Warnell hoped it would provide a hiding place from the angry woman he had impregnated and deserted.

But, regardless of their reasons, once inside the walls of the Alamo, they came together with a common purpose – to defend, even to the death, the principles by which they lived and the great land they hoped would be their future and their legacy.

REFERENCES
1   Hardin, Stephen L., *The Alamo 1836: Santa Anna's Texas Campaign*. Oxford: Osprey Publishing, 2001, p33.

THE MEXICAN ARMY

The Mexican army that arrived in San Antonio de Béxar on February 23, 1836, was beginning a thirteen-day siege that would culminate in a hellish battle on March 6. But they had already marched through hell to reach this place; their journey from San Luis Potosí to the Alamo was a nightmare of exhaustion, deprivation and near-starvation. This ill-equipped, under-trained army marched for weeks through freezing weather and over forbidding terrain. They lived on eight ounces of hardtack or toasted corn cake per day and had water only when they could find it.[1] Some soldiers at least had the company of their families or, perhaps, *soldaderas* (camp followers); but none had the comfort of religious leaders or medical personnel. For the Mexican *soldado*, solace to both body and soul was, at best, inadequate.

Santa Anna's army, in its entirety, consisted of just over six thousand troops; of these, about half were involved in the siege of the Alamo; and of those, perhaps 1,500 participated in the actual assault on March 6.

The great majority of the foot soldiers were conscripts who had been drafted into service – and "drafted" in this case can be read as "kidnapped." The Mexican army routinely raided remote villages to take unmarried men – as well as poor men and prisoners – for a term of up to ten years' service. Often, the wives and children of these men would come along – it was the only way to keep families together. It became the burden of the women to find food and cook it for their families, for even their husbands alone could barely survive on the rations doled out by the army. The troops were also followed by wagons of merchants, with food, dry goods and other necessities available – at highly inflated prices – in exchange for the soldiers' paltry pay.

Officials conscripted Indians, many of whom could not speak a word of Spanish. The Yucatan Battalion, for example, was composed almost entirely of Mayans who must have viewed their predicament with either terror or a kind of numb resignation. They were carelessly uniformed and trained. Because of ammunition conservation, many *soldados* never fired their Brown Bess muskets

Mexikansiches Militär.
Um 1826.

at all until the cold pre-dawn when they attacked the Alamo. It is not certain how many Mexicans fell that morning to "friendly fire" but it can be assumed that many of the frightened Indian villagers-turned-soldiers fired wildly into the darkness, shooting their own comrades in the process.

There were two kinds of infantry battalions: *permanentes*, or regular troops, and *activos*, or conscripts. The *permanentes* were federally funded veterans, well-trained and disciplined, while the *activos* were

ABOVE: *This 1893 German lithograph gives a reasonably authentic overview of the Mexican army uniforms during the Texas Campaign. [Joseph Musso Collection.]*

considered to be little more than cannon fodder. The ten primary infantry battalions (or *tercios*) were named after the heroes of the Mexican Revolution against Spain: Hidalgo, Allende, Morelos, Geurrero, Aldama, Jiminez, Landero, Matamoros, Abasolo and Galeana. Backing them up were eight standing companies: Acapulco, San Blas, Tampico, 1st Bacalar, 2nd Bacalar, Carmen Island, 1st Tabasco and 2nd Tabasco.[2] The *activos* were named after their hometowns or states: Toluca, San Luis, and Queretaro. The cavalry regiments were named for some of the major battles of the Revolution: Dolores, Igula, Palmar, Cuautla, Veracruz, Tampico. The Yucatan and Tabasco regiments were "independent" cavalry units. Each battalion contained two "elite" companies – the grenadiers (*grenaderos*) and light infantrymen (or *cazadores*) – the cream of the army.

Perhaps the premiere regiment of the Mexican army, however, was the *zapadores*, or sappers. Only one hundred and eighty-five strong, this was a crack unit, highly trained and deeply experienced in battle. Primarily engineers, the *zapadores* were also used by Santa Anna as a reserve force in the battle of the Alamo.

The typical firearm of the Mexican army was the British "Brown Bess," a .75-caliber smoothbore musket. While it was a deadly

(continued on page 49)

ABOVE: *General Antonio Lopez de Santa Anna. [Author Collection.]*

MANUEL FERNANDEZ CASTRILLÓN

If the Mexican eyewitness reports of the battle of the Alamo are to be believed, General Manuel Castrillón was one of the bravest, most gallant officers in Santa Anna's army. It is Castrillón who is said to have discovered survivors of the battle. He offered them his protection then took them to Santa Anna as prisoners of war. Santa Anna angrily ordered the prisoners executed immediately.

If the story is true, it was the second time that Castrillón had tried to save the Texians' lives. He had urged Santa Anna to hold off from attacking the Alamo. He believed that if they simply continued to bombard and starve the Texians out that they would eventually surrender, saving not only their own lives (at Santa Anna's "discretion," of course) but the lives of many Mexican soldiers.

Castrillón was Cuban by birth and originally came to Mexico with the invading Spanish army. But he soon switched sides and began serving with Santa Anna in 1822. His intelligence and compassion often put him at odds with Santa Anna, but the general admired Castrillón and relied upon his judgment – when it suited him. Santa Anna believed that a decisive victory at the Alamo was more important, politically at least, than a surrender. Santa Anna and Castrillón disagreed again six weeks later when Castrillón objected to siting their camp at San Jacinto, believing it to be too vulnerable to Sam Houston's army.

Indeed, the Mexican army certainly was in a most vulnerable position at San Jacinto and the result for Santa Anna was defeat, humiliation, and the loss of Texas. For Castrillón, the result was death. Wounded during the attack, he reportedly folded his arms and glared at the advancing Texians who were about to kill him. "I've been in forty battles and never showed my back," he said. "I'm too old to do it now."[7]

MARTÍN PERFECTO DE COS

Martín Perfecto de Cos worked his way toward the top of the Mexican army despite the fact that he was only an average soldier and, perhaps, a poorer than average officer. Nevertheless, he rose swiftly through the ranks from his enlistment in the army in 1820 to the time he was promoted to general in 1833. Alamo folklore insists that this had to do with the fact that Cos was Santa Anna's brother-in-law – in fact, there is no evidence to support the idea that Cos was even married when he served under General Santa Anna.

Cos became one of the prominent figures of the Texas Revolution in 1835 when Santa Anna dispatched him to Anahuac, the port of Galveston Bay to regulate the payment of duties and taxes against which the Texians were chafing. In anticipation of Cos's arrival, William B. Travis gathered twenty-five men and one cannon to conquer the small Mexican garrison under Captain Antonio Tenorio at Anahuac. They quickly forced the Mexicans to surrender.

At this point, however, Texians were still divided on the issue of rebellion; the rival War Party and Peace Party were in constant conflict over how to proceed against the Mexican government. Many in the Peace Party were embarrassed by Travis's actions at Anahuac and even wrote apologies to Cos.

Instead of taking over at Anahuac, Cos moved onto San Antonio de Béxar under Santa Anna's orders. There he was to join Colonel Domingo de Ugartecha, who was at that time fortifying the Alamo mission. This action was seen as hostile, even by the Peace Party. With Cos's entrance into Béxar, no one doubted that war was imminent.

Cos was defeated at the Battle of Béxar in December 1835, and ordered out of Texas. But, marching south, he and his retreating troops met Santa Anna's army in Laredo on the day after Christmas. Although Cos had surrendered under the pledge that he would never again bear arms in Texas, he immediately joined Santa Anna and began the long march back to the Alamo.

Cos proved to be an ineffectual leader during the battle of the Alamo. His under-trained men panicked, broke ranks, fired willy-nilly into the fray, as often as not hitting their fellow soldiers. Some survivors' accounts suggest that Cos ordered the corpses of Crockett and Travis to be mutilated in the aftermath of the battle, but such tales are almost certainly apocryphal.

Cos remained with Santa Anna after the fall of the Alamo and was with him on April 21 at San Jacinto. Like Santa Anna, Cos broke and ran from the scene. He was captured two days later. "Prisoner Cos was said to have been a popular sightseeing attraction for the Americans," writes Thom Hatch, "who were surprised that this famous, dapper general was just a 'little scrub of a thing.'"[5]

When the Texas Revolution ended, Cos remained in the Mexican army, suffering a defeat at Tampico in 1838 and *two* defeats at Tuxpan, in 1839 and again in 1847. Perhaps finally admitting his inadequacies as a military man, Cos went into government work, serving as commandant general and political chief of the Tehuantepec territory.[6] He died in Minatitlan, Vera Cruz, in 1854.

ABOVE: *General Martín Perfecto de Cos, from the book* Pioneer Heroes and Daring Deeds, *Scammell & Company, 1882. [Craig R. Covner Collection.]*

FAR LEFT: *An 1828 lithograph done from life by Claudio Linati of a Mexican soldier from the 1st Battalion in parade dress. The tricolor target was painted on the top of the shako and the winged epaulettes were adapted to distinguish them from the French uniforms from which they were copied. [Courtesy Joseph Musso.]*

LEFT: *An 1828 lithograph done from life by Claudio Linati of a Mexican officer in the Regular Cavalry. [Courtesy Joseph Musso.]*

FAR LEFT: *An 1828 lithograph done from life by Claudio Linati of a lancer from the Mexican presidial companies. [Courtesy Joseph Musso.]*

LEFT: *An 1828 lithograph done from life by Claudio Linati of a Mexican infantryman in the tropical white uniform with the white cloth cover over the shako to protect it from the weather. This style dress was similar to the light gray fatigue uniform worn by all units of the Mexican infantry during the Alamo period when parade dress wasn't called for. [Courtesy Joseph Musso.]*

weapon when handled by an expert – a good marksman could load and fire it four times a minute – many of the Mexican *soldados* had little or no training with the Brown Bess ... or any firearm at all. For close combat, the Brown Bess could be augmented by a triangular-shaped bayonet, which left a nasty, gaping wound that would prove almost impossible to heal.

These weapons, of course, only came into play at the Alamo during the final assault. Throughout the previous twelve days of the siege, the Mexicans hammered away at the Alamo's walls with cannon and howitzers. The artillery contained at least twenty-one such guns. The largest were two cannon that could fire twelve-pound shells. Most of the *(continued on page 55)*

RIGHT: *This ca. 1828 watercolor by Lino Sanchez y Tapia depicts a presidial trooper. [Thomas Gilcrease Institute of American History and Art, Tulsa, Oklahoma.]*

JUAN NEPOMUCENO ALMONTE

Colonel Juan Almonte served as Santa Anna's *aide de camp* and interpreter during the Texas campaign. Of all the Mexican officers, he, perhaps, had led the most eventful life. Born in 1803, Almonte was the illegitimate son of a parish priest, José Morelos y Pavon, and an Indian girl. Little is known about his mother, but Almonte's father was an outspoken revolutionary whose criticism of the government led to his execution in 1815. Almonte was sent to school in New Orleans where he became fluent in English.

Within a few years, he returned to Mexico to join in the country's fight for freedom. He showed talent as an ambassador as well as a soldier and, after the revolution, was sent to England to help work out Mexico's first commercial treaty with a foreign power.

Almonte served in the National Congress and worked as a newspaper editor. In 1834, he embarked on a fact-finding mission through Texas to help establish the border between Texas and the United States. In addition to his official duties, Almonte was also gathering facts of a more explosive kind, taking the political temperature of the region that was already fermenting revolt. When he returned to Mexico, Almonte recommended that Mexico make a greater military presence in Texas, for he believed the area was about to be lost.

At the Alamo, it was "the smooth as syrup"[8] Almonte who met with Travis's emissary, Albert Martin. Standing on the footbridge that spanned the river, Martin suggested that Travis and Almonte could talk things over, but Almonte protested that he had no power to offer any terms to the Texians and that they must surrender the Alamo immediately. It was a demand that Travis answered with a cannon shot.

Almonte was among those officers who urged Santa Anna to hold off from attacking the Alamo, and it may have been he who escorted Susannah Dickinson, Juana Alsbury and the other women of the Alamo to safety after the battle.

He was captured at San Jacinto and was held prisoner for seven months; the Texians remarked on his good humor throughout the ordeal. In 1837, he accompanied Santa Anna to Washington D. C. where they dined with President Andrew Jackson and his cabinet. Later, Almonte served as Mexico's minister of war, then as an ambassador to the United States, and finally, in 1862, as president of Mexico. Unfortunately, he supported Emperor Maximilian; when that regime was overthrown in 1866, Almonte fled to Paris, where he died three years later.

ABOVE: *Standard of the Batallon Matamoros Permanente. Captured at San Jacinto, this standard was also used at the Alamo. [Texas State Library and Archives Commission.]*

LEFT: *Standard of the Batallon Guerrero. Captured at San Jacinto, this standard was also used at the Alamo. [Texas State Library and Archives Commission.]*

ANTONIO LÓPEZ DE SANTA ANNA PÉREZ DE LEBRON

There has been some debate among historians about just how much of a sense of doom was felt by the men of the Alamo over the course of the siege. If they knew anything about the military policies of the man commanding the Mexican army, that sense of doom must have been palpable. General Antonio López de Santa Anna Pérez de Lebron was not known for his *largesse* on the field of battle. On the contrary, Santa Anna was a proponent of total victory, without terms, without mercy. When he demanded of Travis that the garrison surrender "at discretion," he meant their fates were entirely in his hands. And he had proven time and again that the only way to deal with prisoners was to summarily execute them.

The men of the Alamo garrison were "between a rock and a hard place" – if Santa Anna attacked before reinforcements arrived, they would almost certainly die; if they surrendered, he would almost certainly kill them. He had already proven as much only months earlier when he had suppressed a revolt in Zacatecas with a defeat that was virtually a massacre. And he would prove it again, after the Alamo, by ordering the execution of Fannin and all of his men at La Bahía at Goliad.

Santa Anna began forming his military theories in his youth. Born in Jalapa, Vera Cruz, in 1794, Santa Anna joined the army at the age of sixteen. He served as a cadet in the Fio de Cruz infantry regiment under Joaquín de Arredondo, a ruthless commander with a record of merciless, crushing victories. Arredondo suppressed the Miguel Hidalgo y Costilla revolt in 1812, cut a bloody swath through the insurgents in Texas in 1813, and beat José Alvarez de Toledo y Dubois's rebels in the battle of Medina the same year. (Arredondo also had a lasting effect on the history of Texas when, in 1820, he approved Moses Austin's petition to bring settlers into the province. It is ironic that Santa Anna's mentor in effect put into motion the events that would lead to Santa Anna's downfall in 1836.)

Santa Anna was cited for bravery at Medina, and Arredondo seems to have taken the young man under his wing. "In the aftermath of the rebellion," writes Wilfred H. Callcott, "the young officer witnessed Arredondo's fierce counterinsurgency policy of mass executions, and historians have speculated that Santa Anna modeled his policy

and conduct in the Texas Revolution on his experience under Arredondo."[4]

After a series of promotions, Santa Anna, now a brevet lieutenant colonel, served with General Agustín de Iturbide's rebel forces. He distinguished himself to the extent that he was promoted again, to brigadier general. Abruptly, in December 1822 Santa Anna joined the Republican army that opposed Iturbide. The rift between Santa Anna and Iturbide may have been more personal than political – or it may have been, simply, that Santa Anna had the instinct to move over to the winning side. The Republicans eventually forced Iturbide into exile and Santa Anna served as Yucatan's military governor, then as governor of Vera Cruz.

Santa Anna's command against a Spanish force at Tampico in 1829 made him a national hero, which in turn helped him become elected

ABOVE: *General Antonio Lopez de Santa Anna. [Craig R. Covner Collection.]*

president in 1833. He was to serve as Mexico's president six times in all: 1833-35, 1839, 1841-43, 1844, 1847, and 1853-55.

He was one of the authors of the Constitution of 1824 but, once he became president, he decided that Mexico was unprepared for democracy and declared that the Constitution was invalid. The abolishment of the Constitution outraged not only the new Texian settlers, but many thousands of Mexican natives. Liberals in Zacatecas revolted violently against his regime and Santa Anna moved on them swiftly, wiping out the insurrection in a bloody massacre. Then, after General Cos's embarrassing defeat at San Antonio de Béxar, he took it upon himself to

end the Texas Revolution once and for all.

Santa Anna scored a major victory at the Alamo but was himself defeated at San Jacinto some six weeks later. In order to save his own life, he ordered his armies back to Mexico and relinquished Texas, which immediately became an independent republic.

Santa Anna's life after the Texas Revolution was filled with incident. He was still to serve as Mexico's president three more times, lost a leg during the "Pastry War" with France in 1838, and assisted in overthrowing Anastasio Bustamante's government in 1841. He commanded forces during the Mexican War and was defeated at Cerro Gordo by General Winfield Scott.

Despite repeated attempts to return to power, Santa Anna lived out most of the rest of his life in exile, in Cuba and the Dominican Republic. In his final years, he wrote his fascinating, but highly unreliable, memoirs. He returned to Mexico City in 1874 and died there, a pauper, two years later.

Perhaps the oddest footnote to Santa Anna's career came in 1869. In New York, trying to raise money, he sold a ton of chicle to inventor Thomas Adams who wanted to develop it as a rubber substitute. But when Adams noticed that Santa Anna enjoyed chewing the chicle he got the idea of sweetening the substance and marketing it. The new product was a success; hence the Napoleon of the West played a significant role in the invention of chewing gum.

rest were nine-pounders. These were efficient but relatively weak, at least at the range at which they were fired on the Alamo. Although they battered the walls, none of the Mexican shells caused a great deal of damage. Indeed, according to Travis's letters, they never killed a single defender.

With its mix of skilled, professional soldiers and bewildered raw recruits, the Mexican army nevertheless presented an imposing threat to the rebelling colonists in Texas. Dressed splendidly in uniforms inspired by those of Napoleon's French troops, they looked like a real army and, as the unfortunates of Zacatecas could attest, they could deal death like a real army. Minister of War Tornel boasted, "The superiority of the Mexican soldier over the mountaineers of Kentucky and the hunters of Missouri is well known. Veterans seasoned by twenty years of wars can't be intimidated by the presence of an army ignorant of the art of war, incapable of discipline, and renowned for insubordination."[3] And, as they marched into San Antonio de Béxar, banners flying and sabers rattling, it seemed that he was right.

REFERENCES
1   Hardin, Stephen L., *The Alamo, 1836: Santa Anna's Texas Campaign.* Oxford: Osprey Publishing, 2001, p15.
2   Todish, Tim J., and Terry S., *The Alamo Sourcebook 1836.* Austin: Eakin Press, 1998, pp19 and 171.
3   Lord, Walter, *A Time to Stand.* New York: Harper and Brothers, 1961, p68.
4   Wilfred H. Callcott : "Santa Anna, Antonio López de." *The Handbook of Texas Online.* http://www.tsha.utexas.edu/handbook/online.
5   Hatch, Thom, *Encyclopedia of the Alamo and the Texas Revolution.* Jefferson, NC: McFarland & Company, Inc., 1999, p68.
6   Hazlewood, Claudia, "Cos, Martin Perfecto de." *The Handbook of Texas Online.* http://www.tsha.utexas.edu/handbook/online.
7   Hatch, Thom, *Encyclopedia of the Alamo and the Texas Revolution.* Jefferson, NC: McFarland & Company, Inc., 1999, p65.
8   Lord, Walter, *A Time to Stand.* New York: Harper and Brothers, 1961. p104.

THE BATTLE

On the morning of February 23, 1836, the citizens of San Antonio de Béxar were in an uproar. An air of excitement bordering on panic was spreading through the town. Families were packing their belongings into wagons or carts or onto the backs of their mules. Those who had no wagons or carts or mules simply bundled up their possessions, slung them over their shoulders and began scurrying out of town.

Curious and concerned, William Barret Travis sent men to question some of the townspeople, who answered all questions by insisting they were going out into the fields to

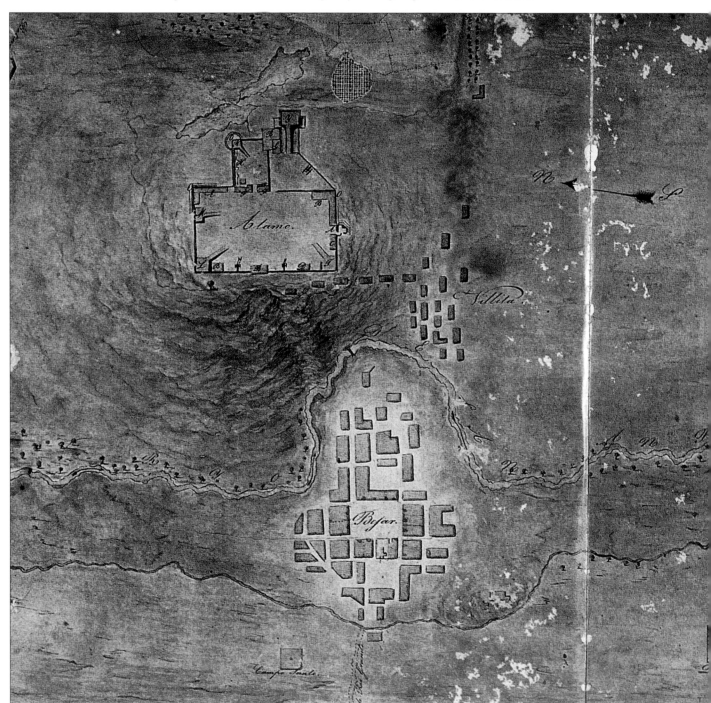

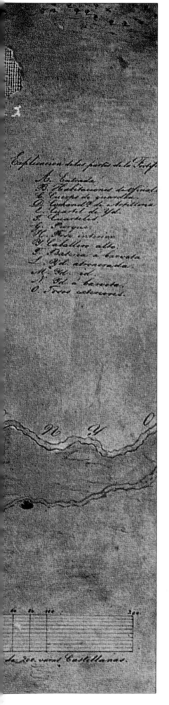

do some farming. Frustrated, Travis ordered the arrest of random citizens, and he interrogated them, hoping to learn what was causing this mass exodus. Finally, he was told the truth – Santa Anna had arrived. His cavalry was a mere eight miles away. The night before, the general had sent a messenger into Béxar, warning the citizens to get out of town before the violence began.

"It would have been easy enough to have surprised [the town]," Santa Anna later wrote, "because those occupying it did not have the faintest news of the march of our army." He had ordered General Joaquin Ramírez y Sesma to attack earlier, but said that Ramírez y Sesma misunderstood these "concise and definite" orders and simply waited for Santa Anna to arrive. "This, perhaps, was the result of inevitable circumstances," Santa Anna wrote philosophically; "and although the city was captured, the surprise that I had ordered to be carried out would have saved the time consumed and the blood shed later in the taking of the Alamo."[1]

Actually, there was a good reason why Ramírez y Sesma had not attacked earlier. Only the night before, most of the citizens of Béxar had been whooping it up at a fandango honoring George Washington's birthday. The timing would have been perfect to sweep into town and wipe out the Texians while their guard was down – and their liquor consumption was up. But a driving rainstorm had swept across the area, causing a significant rise in the Medina River, making it impossible for Ramírez y Sesma to attack.

THE ENEMY IN VIEW

Travis didn't want to believe that Santa Anna had come so far so fast. A march through northern Mexico in the dead of winter seemed incredibly foolhardy – as, indeed it had been. The Mexican army endured terrible suffering and privation on the march. They traveled with inadequate supplies of food and water and hardly any medical personnel at all. Some starved, some deserted, and many of them froze to death in the first snow they had ever seen. But Santa Anna – who traveled in relative luxury at the head of his army – had urged his men on for just that reason: because the Texians would never expect it. Now Travis had only to confirm that what he had been told was true. Soon, a desperate pealing of bells from the San Fernando Cathedral tower told him that it was. A sentry in the tower had seen Mexican cavalry banners. "The enemy are in view!" he shouted.

Travis immediately ordered all Texians in Béxar to head toward the Alamo. Captain Almeron Dickinson rode frantically to his home and called out to his wife Susannah to hand him their baby Angelina, then swing onto his horse. James Bowie rushed to the Veramendi Palace to fetch his sisters-in-law, Juana Alsbury and Gertrudis Navarro, into the safety of the fort. Soon, the footbridge over the river and the path to the Alamo was crowded with men, women and children. Captain Juan Seguín marched down Potero Street (now Commerce Street) with his company of *Tejanos* while women shouted, "Poor fellows, you will all be killed, what shall we do?"[2]

Once inside the Alamo, the men scrambled to their posts, while the women went about preparing quarters for themselves and their families. Travis and Bowie drafted a letter:

COMMANDANCY OF BÉXAR

We have removed all the men to the Alamo where we make such resistance as is due our honor, and that of the country, until we can get assistance from you, which we expect you to forward immediately. In this extremity, we hope you will send us all the men you can spare promptly. We have one hundred and forty six men, who are determined never to retreat.

The letter was clearly written by Travis, making use of some of his favorite phrases. But the fact that it was signed by both commanders of the Alamo is significant. Whatever differences they may have had earlier on were no longer an issue.

As the Texians occupied the Alamo, Santa Anna and his army swept into Béxar with pomp and ceremony. Travis felt that the marching troops provided an easy target, and as soon as they reached the plaza in front of the San Fernando Cathedral he ordered a cannon shot. The shell did no real damage, and the Mexicans quickly returned fire with four howitzer grenades.

At the same time, a group of Mexican soldiers raised an ominous flag over the San Fernando Cathedral. Red as blood and perhaps even decorated with a skull and crossbones, the flag's meaning was evident to all in the Alamo – no quarter. If the men of the Alamo surrendered, they would have to do so on Santa Anna's terms.

Despite – or perhaps because of – the red flag, both Travis and Bowie made separate

57

LEFT: *Juan N. Seguín, Tejano leader, later mayor of San Antonio who left the Alamo as a courier and commanded a company of Texas natives at the battle of San Jacinto. [Stephen L. Hardin Collection.]*

BELOW: *The banner of the New Orleans Greys, the only surviving flag known to have flown over the Alamo during the siege. [Texas State Library & Archives Commission.]*

attempts to parlay with Santa Anna. Bowie's note to Santa Anna suggests that he wanted to work out a solution before things got out of hand: "Because a shot was fired from a cannon of this fort at the time a red flag was raised over the tower of San Fernando, and because a little afterward they told me that a part of your army had sounded a parlay, which was not heard before the firing of the shot. I wish, Sir, to ascertain if it be true that a parley was called ..."

Green B. Jameson took the message to the river under a flag of truce. He was met there on the footbridge by Colonel Juan Almonte, Santa Anna's *aide de camp*. Almonte politely told Jameson that he had no authority to discuss terms and suggested that the Texians should simply surrender at discretion.

Later, Albert Martin approached Almonte at Travis's behest, suggesting that Travis would be willing to receive him "with much pleasure" for a parlay. Almonte repeated what he had told Jameson.

Soon, Bowie received a message from Colonel Don José Batres, another of Santa Anna's *aides de camp*: "... the Mexican army cannot come to terms under any conditions with rebellious foreigners to whom there is no other recourse left, if they wish to save their lives, than to place themselves immediately at the disposal of the Supreme Government from whom alone they may expect clemency after some considerations are taken up. God and Liberty."[3]

Travis's reply to this note was swift and succinct – a single cannon shot. That shot

LEFT: *The items in this photo are some of the many artifacts from Joseph Musso's extensive collection. All are original, except where noted, and all are related to (or existed prior to) the fall of the Alamo.*

1 *Original glazed leather yeoman style shako mounted with the brass losange style shako plate bearing the Mexican eagle, brass trim all around the bill, and the Mexican tricolor painted on top.*

2 *Gold scale Mexican officer's epaulets bearing gold leaf relief Mexican eagle on the button.*

3 *Mexican cavalry saber, ca. 1835, with a sharkskin-wrapped grip and the Mexican eagle cast in relief on the guard.*

4 *Third model, India Land Pattern British "Brown Bess" musket, dated 1810 on the lock with faint traces of the Mexican eagle and restocked in Mexican wood during the period. (The white buff sling is a modern reproduction.)*

5 *"Kentucky rifle" made in about 1816, and used in many Alamo movies.*

6 *Mexican officer's metal military notebook binder with the Mexican eagle overlaid on the front.*

7 *Scientifically tested ca. 1830 Bowie knife with the initials "J.B" on the crossguard quillon along with a six-pointed, pre-1850 American officer's star of the period. It has a 13 ³/₄ in long blade, 2 ⁷/₁₆ in wide, ¹/₄ in thick, with an overlaid sheet brass strip sweat-soldered on the back. The handle is ebonized hardwood. Sam Houston was pictured using this knife during the Alamo period in an illustration from the book* The Life of Sam Houston: The Only Authentic Memoir of Him Ever Written *(1855 edition), see photo on page 1 of this book, which also shows Bowie's letter from the Alamo to Santa Anna. [Letter on page 1 courtesy of the Bienecke Library, Yale University; knife and book courtesy of Joseph Musso.]*

8 *"Guardless coffin" handled knife mounted in sheets of coin silver with burl walnut grips. The blade is about 9 ¹/₄ in long, 1 ¹/₂ in wide.*

9 *American-made Bowie knife, ca. 1834, mounted in German silver with ebony grips. The blade is 11 ⁵/₈ in long, 2 in wide and ³/₁₆ in thick. It is identical to one that was allegedly picked up on the San Jacinto battlefield shortly after the battle.*

10 *U.S. 1821 Contract American officer's gold-gilt eagle-headed sword with mother-of-pearl grips, and the Roman goddess Victoria cast in the counter guard. The sword is almost identical to the one still owned by James Bowie's descendant which family history maintains is the eagle-headed object that Bowie is holding in his portrait (see page 36).*

11 *U.S. Military belt buckle from the War of 1812.*

12 *Booklet,* Siege of the Alamo: A Mexico-Texan Tale *(1888) by W. S. Heavenhill.*

13 *Copy of Davy Crockett's 1837 Almanack of* Wild Sports in the West, Life in the Backwoods, and Sketches of Texas, *Vol.1 No. 3 published by the heirs of Colonel Crockett in Nashville, Tennessee.*

almost immediately became a part of Travis's legend, a potent symbol of his bravery and determination; an indelible sign – a day before he actually wrote it in a letter – that he would "never surrender or retreat."

But Santa Anna was both perplexed and annoyed by Travis's furious reply. "That conflict of arms was bloody, because the chief Travis, who commanded the forces of the Alamo, would not enter into any capitulation, and his responses were insulting," Santa Anna later wrote. "The obstinacy of Travis and his

ABOVE: *Theodore Gentilz's meticulous (and, it must be admitted, rather lifeless)* Fall of the Alamo *(1885), long considered among the most accurate of Alamo paintings. Many of Gentilz's architectural and military details are mistaken, however. The original oil painting was destroyed as the result of a fire; only monochrome copies are now known to exist. [Library of Congress.]*

RIGHT: *Travis delivers his answer to Santa Anna's demand for surrender. Actually, since this is a* Classics Illustrated *comic about Davy Crockett, Travis lets Davy do the honors. [Author Collection.]*

soldiers was the cause of the death of the whole of them, for not one would surrender."[4]

Travis had fired the opening shot of the siege, but the Mexican army replied with a continuing barrage of shells. At Santa Anna's orders, they began bombarding the Alamo around the clock, trying relentlessly to batter down the walls.

Travis knew that his situation was dire and that reinforcements must arrive soon or the Texas Revolution would be over before it started. It was on the second day of the siege, under the cacophony of cannon shots and the unceasing music from Santa Anna's bands, that Travis wrote a letter for help that would become his epistle to every ensuing generation of Texans:

COMMANDANCY OF THE ALAMO, BÉXAR, FEB'Y. 24TH, 1836.

To the People of Texas & All Americans in the world – –
Fellow citizens and compatriots –

I am besieged by a thousand or more of the Mexicans under Santa Anna – – I have sustained a continual bombardment & cannonade for 24 hours & have not lost a man – the enemy has demanded a surrender at discretion, otherwise the garrison are to be put to the sword, if the fort is taken – I have answered the demand with a cannon shot, and our flag still waves proudly from the walls – I shall never surrender or retreat. Then, I call on you in the name of Liberty, of patriotism & everything dear to the American character to come to our aid with all dispatch – The enemy is receiving reinforcements daily and will no doubt increase to three or four thousand in four or five days. If this call is neglected, I am determined to sustain myself as long as possible & die like a soldier who never forgets what is due to his own honor and that of his country.

Victory or death.

William Barret Travis
Lt. Colonel Comdt.

P. S. The Lord is on our side – when the enemy appeared in sight we had not three bushels of corn – we have since found in deserted houses 80 or 90 bushels & got into the walls 20 or 30 head of Beeves.

Travis

This letter, unlike that of the day before, was not co-signed by Bowie. His illness had suddenly worsened and he had been removed to a room in the *Galera*, or Low Barracks. There is no way to determine the precise nature of Bowie's illness. It is known that he had previously suffered from malaria and may have been suffering a relapse. Others suggest that he had typhoid or, perhaps, tuberculosis. At any rate, from this point on, Bowie ceased to function as one of the commanders of the Alamo; in fact, he may have ceased to play a role of any kind in the Alamo siege. Illness had perhaps transformed the great fighter into a noncombatant. (None of Travis's letters from this point on mentions Bowie. This was probably simple prudence; should any of the letters have been captured, he wouldn't have wanted it known that one of the fort's commanders – and one well known by the Mexican army – was incapacitated.)

Travis sent his letter out with courier Albert Martin who scribbled on the back: "Since the above was written I heard a very heavy Canonade during the whole day think there must have been an attack made upon the alamo. We were short of Amunition when I left Hurry on all the men you can in haste."

In Gonzales, Martin passed the note along to Launcelot Smither, who added his own post script: "I hope Every one will Randeves at gonzales as soon as poseble as the Brave Solders are suffering do no neglect the powder it is very scarce and should not be delad one moment."

The appeal did bring one response. On the night of March 1, thirty men from Gonzales, along with Alamo couriers Albert Martin and John Smith, slipped through enemy lines and into the fort. Enrique Esparza, a little boy in the Alamo with his family, remembered years later that when "Sénor Smith came from Gonzales with the band of men he had gathered, there was great shouting. The Texians beat drums and played on a flute."[5] The arrival of these thirty-two reinforcements raised the total in the Alamo to about 189. Oddly, two days later, on March 3, Travis wrote a letter in which he put the number of men in the fort at 145.

PRE-BATTLE SKIRMISHES

The Mexicans spent each day digging trenches and creating cannon emplacements, ever nearer to the Alamo. Although hundreds of shells fell inside the compound, the Alamo garrison had not suffered a single loss. For the men of the garrison, the siege was mostly a waiting game, hoping for reinforcements and dodging Mexican shells. There were only occasional flashes of fighting between the two forces. On February 25, about 300 Mexicans occupied some *jacales* in La Villita about 100 yards from the Alamo, to the south. The next day, the Texians rained down a barrage of gunfire on the *jacales* and made the Mexicans withdraw. That night a few men went out under cover of darkness to burn some of the huts that might afford protection to the Mexicans. The same day, some Mexican

FOLLOWING PAGE: *Armand Welcker's illustration* The Mexican Assault on the Alamo *appeared in the 1888 book* Story of the Wild West and Camp-Fire Chats. *Both the Alamo church and the town of San Antonio loom over the action like skyscrapers while the mob of Texian defenders seems to outnumber their attackers. [Author Collection.]*

cavalry attacked the rear of the fort, at the horse corrals, but were handily repulsed by the Texians.

The weather was cold; the temperature rarely rose above the mid-thirties during the day. At their posts on the Alamo walls, the men were probably quite miserable; especially as they watched Mexican reinforcements arrive almost daily and had to endure the constant din and danger of bombardment. On March 2, their spirits might have risen had they known that the delegation at Washington-on-the-Brazos had declared independence from Mexico on that day. But this news would have been tempered by that of the tragic end, the same day, of Dr. James Grant, who had earlier left the Alamo with the Matamoros Expedition. Grant was ambushed by General Urrea at Agua Dulce Creek and he and fifteen of the men with him were killed.

But the men in the Alamo had no news, good or bad. They only had speculation and worry.

The next day, courier James Butler Bonham arrived to give them some cause for hope. Bonham carried with him a note from Major Robert McAlpin Williamson – called "Three-Legged Willie" because of a peg-leg he wore under one knee – urging Travis to hold out for just a little while longer. "Sixty men have left this municipality, who in all probability are with you by this date," Williamson wrote. "Colonel Fannin with 300 men and four pieces of artillery has been on the march towards Béxar three days now. Tonight we await 300 reinforcements … *For God's sake hold out until we can assist you.*"

The "sixty men" mentioned by Williamson may indeed have arrived at the Alamo on or

(continued on page 70)

BELOW: *This 19th Century picture has remained one of the most popular images of the battle, perhaps because it reconciles the current appearance of the Alamo with its status as a fort. Totally inaccurate and anachronistic, the image nevertheless retains its mythic power. This version is in color, unlike the original. [Author Collection.]*

TRAVIS'S LINE IN THE SAND

It is the shining moment of the Alamo myth. William Barret Travis, knowing that no help was coming, gathers his men together to give them the chance to save their lives – or to sacrifice themselves on the altar of Texas independence. He carefully outlines their desperate situation in terms highly reminiscent of – and only slightly less dramatic than – the "St. Crispin's Day" speech in *Henry V*. Then, he draws a long line in the sand with his saber. Travis invites all those who would stay and defend the Alamo to the death to cross the line. Anyone who wants to leave may do so with all honor.

Young Tapley Holland is the first to leap over the line. His hand over his heart, he cries, "I am willing to die for Texas!" The others follow. Even James Bowie, sick unto death, calls out, "Boys, lift my cot across that line!" Only Louis "Moses" Rose opts out. A former Napoleonic soldier, he has already survived battles like Waterloo, and isn't willing to die defending an old mud fort in Texas. The others, unresentful, wish him a fond farewell and he leaps over the wall.

QUESTIONING THE STORY

There is only one problem with the story of Travis and his line in the sand – we have no reason to believe it happened. Such a gesture was certainly not beyond Travis; he was known to be highly dramatic. And there may have been a recent precedent: some recalled that when the first hero of the revolution called out, "Who will follow old Ben Milam into San Antonio?" Milam drew a line in the sand with the butt of his rifle.

But for Travis to do such a thing, he would have had to be sure that he and his garrison were doomed. Was he? Perhaps not. The standard story is that James Butler Bonham rode bravely through the Mexican lines to deliver his dark message: "Fannin isn't coming. There will be no help." But Bonham may have brought a quite different message.

In 1987 historian Thomas Ricks Lindley discovered a document that changes the entire complexion of the last days of the Alamo. It is a letter to Travis from Major R. M. Williamson (better known as "Three-Legged Willie") dated March 1, 1836. Discovered among Travis's papers after the fall of the Alamo, it was released as a broadside in Mexico on March 31, 1836.[6] The letter reads:

You cannot conceive my anxiety: today it has been four whole days that we have not the slightest news relative to your dangerous situation and we are therefore given over to a thousand conjectures regarding you. Sixty men have left this municipality, who in all probability are with you by this date. Colonel Fannin with 300 men and four pieces of artillery has been on the march towards Béxar three days now. Tonight we await 300 reinforcements from Washington, Bastrop, Brazoria and S. Felipe and no time will be lost in providing you assistance. [...] P.S. For God's sake hold out until we can assist you. – I remit to you with major Bonham a communication from the interim governor. Best wishes to all your people and tell them to hold on firmly by their 'wills' until I go there.
– Williamson
– Write us very soon.

Williamson's letter means that Bonham entered the Alamo on about March 3 with good news – or at least encouraging news. At any time, nearly 700 men would be arriving to help Travis hold the fort. Those reinforcements and the firepower they would bring with them, might just be enough to hold Santa Anna at bay indefinitely – or at least until Houston could get there with the rest of his army.

Admittedly, Travis was skeptical about the message. On March 3, the day that Bonham arrived back at the Alamo, Travis wrote, "Colonel Fannin is said to be on the march to this place with reinforcements; but I fear it is not true, as I have repeatedly sent to him for aid without receiving any." But we have no credible evidence to suggest that Travis relayed his misgivings to his men. It may have been a dramatic gesture to make but it would also have been counterproductive, helping to drain their spirits of hope.

No Alamo survivor ever mentioned such an event until many years later, when William Zuber wrote his highly flavored account of Moses Rose's tale.[7] In that account, Zuber claims that Rose had told the story to Zuber's parents and that they, in turn, had passed it on to him. Thirty-five years later, he wrote down what he could remember and simply invented the rest. Zuber recalled in a letter dated September 14, 1877, "I found a deficiency in

LAST SPEECH OF TRAVIS TO THE GARRIS

the material of the speech, which from my knowledge of [Travis] I thought I could supply. I accordingly threw in one paragraph which I firmly believe to be characteristic of Travis, and without which the speech would have been incomplete." Could that "one paragraph" be the part about "the line"?

It was only after Zuber's account appeared that other Alamo survivors began mentioning "the line." Enrique Esparza didn't talk about it until 1902. Susanna Dickinson didn't bring it up until 1881 – and she had the story reversed: whoever wanted to *leave* should cross the line. "But one stepped out," she recalled. "His name to the best of my recollection was Ross."

Gradually the story of the line began appearing in history books and school texts and soon it was an inextricable part of the Alamo legend – even if historians have always had a hard time believing it.

But legends have their own uses. This one gives a dramatic heart to the story, a specific moment of decision – and decision is what the legend of the Alamo is all about; the whole myth rises or falls on the deliberate choice of the heroes of the Alamo to sacrifice themselves for the good of Texas. Without "the line," the battle of the Alamo is just a chaotic, bloody event of horror and death without the ennobling, quasi-religious element of willing martyrdom. Without "the line," we must redefine the very meaning of the Alamo. Revisionist historians, of course, are trying to do that all the time. But those who want their legends a bit more pristine could do worse than to heed Walter Lord on this one: "As matters stand, there's still room to speculate, and every good Texan can follow the advice of J. K. Beretta in the *Southwest Historical Quarterly*: 'Is there any proof that Travis didn't draw the line? If not, then let us believe it.'"[8]

LEFT: *Louis Eyth's* Last Speech of Travis to his Men at the Alamo, *in pencil. [James T. DeShields Collection, San Antonio, Texas.]*

around March 4. Historian Thomas Ricks Lindley has found evidence suggesting that David Crockett left the fort a few days prior to this and led the group in. If true, the strength of the Alamo was somewhere around 250 men. Much better than the 189 defenders usually accepted by history – but still not nearly enough to defend the sprawling fort against Santa Anna's attack.

And that attack was imminent. On the night of March 5, Santa Anna ordered his officers to make ready for an attack early the next morning. Each column was to be equipped with ladders, crowbars, and axes to help them scale walls and break through doors and barricades. Even though the weather was bitter cold, the *soldados* were forbidden to wear overcoats or to carry blankets "or anything that may impede the rapidity of their motions" – and every man was ordered to wear shoes or sandals.

The troops were ordered to sleep at dusk and were to be awakened at midnight to prepare for the attack. But not every *soldado* would be participating in the battle: "Recruits deficient in instructions will remain in their quarters."

Colonel Joaquin Ramírez y Sesma's cavalry would not join in the attack. Instead, they would ride the perimeter, keeping a lookout for any Texians who might attempt to flee from the fort.

SANTA ANNA CONTEMPT

Many of his officers urged General Santa Anna not to attack. They reasoned that the bombardment and siege would soon either wear the Texians down or starve them into surrender. With patience, the Alamo could easily be taken with no further loss of Mexican life. However, Captain Fernando Urissa recalled that Santa Anna treated such pleas with contempt: "Santa Anna was holding in his hand the leg of a chicken which he was eating and, holding it up, he said,

BELOW: *This 1953 fiesta painting by Ruth Conerly Zachrisson depicts the last moments of William Barret Travis. This exciting battle scene hung for years in the Alamo shrine. [DRT Library, The Alamo.]*

'What are the lives of [our] soldiers than so many chickens?'"[9]

Santa Anna ordered the bombardment to cease. After almost two weeks of deafening, nerve-wracking noise, this silence was like a dream come true for the men of the Alamo. Too exhausted to be suspicious, many fell into a deep sleep. Travis stationed three sentries outside the walls to alert the fort of any attack by the Mexican army. They must have been killed quietly and quickly, for they raised no alarm.

By 3:00 a.m. on March 6, 1836, the Mexican forces were ready. The *soldados* shivered on the ground for two uncomfortable hours as they waited for the order to attack. Then, with a flash of light, several rockets ascended into the sky. Blaring bugles sounded the call to attack. A cheer of "Viva Santa Anna!" swept through the army and, at the orders from their officers, the *soldados* sprang up from their places and began running toward hell.

From the first sounds of the charge, the men of the Alamo sprang to their posts. Travis was awakened in his room on the west wall and as he ran toward a cannon, his slave Joe close behind, he shouted, "Come on, boys. The Mexicans are upon us and we'll give them hell!" Then he shouted, perhaps so the Mexicans would hear and understand, "*No rendirse, muchachos*!" ("No surrender, boys!") But that was all he said. After discharging his shotgun into the crowd of *soldados* crowding the base of the wall, Travis was hit by a single musket ball in the forehead. The twenty-six-year-old commander of the Alamo was perhaps the first man in the garrison to die. Joe watched his master expire then ran to hide.

ABOVE: *The first published depiction of the Battle of the Alamo – in 1837 – gives no sense of what the Alamo looked like, but is a valuable period view, nonetheless. The Alamo defender at the center of the picture is not dressed in buckskins and coonskin cap, but as a normal citizen of 1836 would be dressed. [Author Collection.]*

RIGHT: Siege of the Alamo *by Lajos Markos. This large oil painting makes up in excitement and drama what it lacks in historical authenticity. [Lajos Markos and the Texas State Capitol.]*

II. Texas a Republic; Its Admission to the Union; the Resulting War with Mexico

Texas Declares Its Independence from Mexico. *The Alamo. Sam Houston Defeats Santa Anna.* Although the

Battle of the Alamo, San Antonio, Texas

Americans were only about one fourth of the Texas population, they revolted against Mexico and set up an independent government in 1836. Santa Anna, the president of Mexico, hearing of their action, marched northward to punish the "rebels." At the Alamo, an old mission at

OPPOSITE PAGE: *Many illustrators assume that the Alamo church is and was the Alamo in its entirety. This Mexican cannon crew from* The History of the American People *(1918) is firing from a vantage point that is actually within the grounds of the fort. Illustration by George E. Richards. [Author Collection.]*

LEFT: *The last moments of James Bowie are caught dramatically, if with considerable license, in this illustration by Charles A. Stephens from William O. Stoddard's* The Lost Gold of the Montezumas: A Story of the Alamo. *[London: Henry Frowde, Hodder and Stoughton, 1898.]*

LEFT: *Davy Crockett (Robert Barrat) swings Ol' Betsy at an attacking Mexican soldier in* Man of Conquest (1939), *a motion picture biography of Sam Houston.* [Republic Pictures.]

LEFT: *Although the debate continues to rage regarding the precise nature of David Crockett's death at the Alamo, true Crockett believers consider this to be the most appropriate demise for their hero:* The Battle of the Alamo *(1913) by Frederick Yohn. [Continental Insurance.]*

At first, the men of the Alamo more than held their own. Their cannon, loaded with horseshoes, nails or any kind of scrap metal, cut a horrible swath through the attacking Mexicans. An anonymous soldier later wrote, "The fire from the enemy's cannon was fearful … more than forty men fell around me in a few moments."[10]

Colonel Juan Morales led a small group of about one hundred men against the south wall. General Cos and his battalion found themselves in a delicate position at the west wall – they were fired on both by the Texians and, mistakenly, by some confused *soldados* in the Toluca companies. The same thing happened on the north wall. The *zapadores*

fired at the Texians in order to give the Mexican infantry an opening to go up and over the ruined wall – but many of the shots fell short and killed Mexicans instead of Texians. The "friendly fire" almost turned the scene into chaos. Many *soldados* seemed ready to abandon the fight and run for their lives. But General Juan Amador began climbing the wall, calling to his men to follow him into the Alamo. The brave gesture seemed to inspire the *soldados* and they began to climb up, using the chinks and holes in the ragged wall as hand and footholds.

Now the Texians began to abandon the north and west walls as the Mexicans poured into the compound, as Joe later put it, "like sheep." They had fortified the rooms of the Long Barracks and it was there to which they ran. On the way, the defenders fought savagely, using their empty rifles as clubs, slashing with their great knives, selling their lives as dearly as possible. Those who didn't make it into the Long Barracks in time, or those foolhardy enough to try to fight it out in the Plaza, were soon cut down.

Although the rooms of the Long Barracks had been fortified, the Texians apparently hadn't counted on one thing – their cannon were still outside and still operable. The Mexicans simply turned them around and began blowing apart the doors of the Long Barracks. Those blasts must have killed off most of the men inside; then, *soldados* with swords and bayonets rushed into the rooms to finish the job.

On the second floor of the Long Barracks, the sick and wounded of the Alamo lay in the hospital, listening to the sounds of battle growing ever nearer. Suddenly, several Mexicans burst in and began slaughtering the defenseless men. The same thing happened down in the Low Barracks where more sick and wounded lay – including James Bowie. There is no reliable account that tells how Bowie met his end, but because he was ill and bedridden, some who recognized him assumed the worst. "... that perverse and haughty James Bowie," wrote one anonymous soldier, "died like a woman, in bed, almost hidden by the covers."[11]

David Crockett and the Tennessee Mounted Volunteers may have been stationed at the wood-and-earth palisade that connected the church to the Low Barracks. (The only eyewitness account that places Crockett at this particular place is that of John Sutherland, who claimed to have left the Alamo as a

(continued on page 84)

THE EXECUTION OF SURVIVORS

The Alamo is seen as the prototypical "last stand" in which every man, having vowed to die for Texas, fought to his last breath. Reality, however, is rarely as neat as myth and there were almost certainly a few survivors of the battle who were executed after the fact. Though this has happened in thousands of battles throughout history, for some reason the Alamo faithful reject the possibility that it could have happened among that pristine band of martyrs. And the suggestion that Davy Crockett, king of the wild frontier, was among them is almost too much to bear.

Although it is nearly certain that the executions took place, almost every other detail is up for debate – including the presence of Crockett. Captain Fernando Urissa saw the murder of "a venerable old man" whom General Castrillón tried to save. Urissa recalled that "Santa Anna replied, 'What right have you to disobey my orders? I want no prisoners,' and waving his hand to a file of soldiers he said, Soldiers, shoot that man,' and almost instantly he fell, pierced with a volley of balls. Castrillón turned aside with tears in his eyes..." Urissa asked the old man's name and was told it was "Coket."

Antonio Cruz y Arrocha, a San Antonian who lived near the Alamo, claimed that several Texians approached Santa Anna and "kneeled, each one holding a small white flag." Santa Anna saw them and made a sign to his soldiers, and "they were immediately showered by bayonet stabs."

Manuel Loranca, a Mexican lieutenant, remembered seeing the corpses of Bowie and Travis before entering a "corridor which served the Texians as quarters and here found all refugees which were left. President Santa Anna immediately ordered that they should be shot, which was accordingly done."

Another officer, José Juan Sanchez Navarro, was "horrified by some cruelties, among others, the death of an old man named Cochran and a boy of about fourteen."

And another, Francisco Becerra, told of finding Travis and Crockett alive in a room "sitting on the floor among feathers." Becerra claimed that Travis offered him money to let him go, but they were both brought before Santa Anna. They were both shot and, according to Becerra, they "died undaunted, like heroes."

Ramón Martinez Caro, Santa Anna's secretary, saw five prisoners executed. He also claimed that they were protected by Castrillón, who was "severely reprimanded" by Santa Anna "for not having killed them." As Castrillón stood by, some of Santa Anna's soldiers "stepped out of their ranks, and set upon the prisoners until they were all killed."[14]

But by far the most controversial report of such executions came from Colonel José Enrique de la Peña, a lieutenant in the *zapadores* battalion. Peña kept a journal throughout the Texas campaign and in later years began embellishing it with other reports. There is an ongoing controversy about the legitimacy of this document, but if it is genuine, it is one of the most valuable records of the Texas Revolution in existence.[15]

Peña described the event this way:

"Some seven men had survived the general massacre and guided by General Castrillón, who protected them, were presented to Santa Anna. Among them was one of great stature, well-formed and with regular features, in whose face was stamped the pain of adversity, but in which could be observed a certain resignation and dignity which spoke well of him. It was the naturalist [or 'outdoorsman'? – naturalista] David Croket, very well known in North America for his novel adventures, who had come to examine the country and who, happening to be in Béjar in the moments of surprise, had confined himself in the Alamo, fearful of not being respected in his capacity as a foreigner. Santa Anna answered the intervention of Castrillón with a gesture of indignation, and addressing himself immediately to the sappers [the zapadores – de la Peña's unit during the invasion of Texas], which was the soldiery he had nearest, ordered that they shoot them. The junior and senior officers became indignant at this action and did not repeat the command, hoping that with the passing of the first moment of fury, those men would be saved; but different officers who were around the President and who perhaps had not been there in the moment of danger, made themselves conspicuous by a despicable act; surpassing them in cruelty, they pushed themselves forward to them, in order to flatter the [cruelty?]

of their commander, and sword in hand they threw themselves on those unhappy defenseless men, in the same way that a tiger leaps upon its prey. They tortured them before they killed them, and these miserable ones died moaning, but without humbling themselves before their executioners. It is said that General Ramírez y Sesma was one of them: I do not testify to it, because although I was present, I averted my gaze with horror, so as not to see such a barbarous scene."[16]

Although none of the accounts really matches up with another – various eyewitness report one, two, five and seven prisoners – it seems probable that at least some of the Alamo's defenders lived through the battle and were executed afterward, either by gunshot or sword. Whether Crockett was among them remains more controversial than the matter should be.

ABOVE: *Without firm evidence, the nature of David Crockett's demise has been the subject of much literary and visual conjecture. Here is a rather serene depiction of his last moments as seen in a painting in the National Historical War Museum in Washington, D.C. [Author Collection.]*

courier midway through the siege. Since new evidence shows that Sutherland left the Alamo early February 19, before the siege began, serious doubts have been cast upon his entire story. If it proves to be untrue, then there is nothing at all to substantiate the claim that Crockett defended the palisade.) Several accounts purport to tell the story of Crockett's last moments – in ways that range from clubbing dozens of Mexicans with his broken gun – and broken arm – to surrendering after the fight, only to be executed. But there is nothing at all which actually stands up as evidence.[12]

The only thing certain is that David Crockett died that morning in the Alamo, among his comrades. (For a more thorough discussion of the various Crockett death stories, see box feature "The Execution of Survivors" page 82.)

DEATH IN THE CHURCH

Inside the Alamo church, the families of some of the Alamo's defenders huddled, trembling in fear. Eight year-old Enrique Esparza could see his father Gregorio at his post on a cannon ramp at the back of the church.

Lieutenant Almeron Dickinson may have been at that post, as well. Susannah and Angelina, his wife and baby daughter, waited out the battle in their quarters in the sacristy. Now, the Alamo church received the full attention of the Mexicans. The defenders' cannon crew at the top of the ramp must have done the best they could, but the Mexicans surging through the church door quickly wiped them out. Two young, unarmed boys, perhaps the sons of defender Anthony Wolfe, were killed. But Enrique Esparza and his family were spared.

Susannah Dickinson reported that one man rushed into the room where she was, looking for a place to hide. He was quickly followed in by several Mexican soldiers who killed him, but then callously proceeded to toss his body on their bayonets "as a bundle of fodder."[13]

Even after the day was clearly won, Mexican soldiers continued firing and hacking at the corpses of the Texians. They even shot a cat, claiming that it wasn't just a cat, but "an American." But that cat wasn't the last "American" to die. A few survivors, hurt and exhausted, were found. General Castrillón gallantly offered to protect them. But when he brought them before Santa Anna, the Napoleon of the West angrily reminded Castrillón of his orders of no quarter. The dictator demanded that the survivors be executed. Several of Santa Anna's guard, who had not participated in the battle, leapt forward and hacked the unfortunate men to pieces with their swords.

Now, the battle of the Alamo was finally over, little more than an hour after it began. Santa Anna toured the scene, asking to be shown the bodies of Travis, Bowie, and Crockett. He considered the storming of the Alamo to be a great victory – but not *too* great. "It was," he said, "a small affair."

REFERENCES

1 Castaneda, Carlos Eduardo, *The Mexican Side of the Texan Revolution by the Chief Mexican Participants*. Austin: Graphic Ideas Inc., 1970, pp12-13.

2 Teja, Jesus F. de la, *A Revolution Remembered: The Memoirs and Selected Corrrespondence of Juan n. Seguín*. Austin: State House Press, 1991, p194.

3 Archivo General de Mexico Papers, University of Texas at Austin. Jose Batres to James Bowie, February 23, 1836.

4 Letter to Henry A. McCardle, March 19, 1874.

5 Driggs, Howard R., and Sarah S. King, *Rise of the Lone Star: A Story of Texas Told by its Pioneers*. New York: Frederick A. Stokes Company, 1936, p223.

6 *The Alamo Journal*, #62, August 1988: article: "James Butler Bonham" by Thomas Ricks Lindley.

7 Zuber, William, "An Escape From the Alamo" published in *The Texas Almanac*, 1873, pp80-85.

8 Lord, Walter, *A Time to Stand*. New York: Harper & Brothers, 1961, p204.

9 Huffines, Alan, with Gary Zaboly, *The Blood of Noble Men*. Austin: Eakin Press, 1999, p115.

10 *El Mosquito Mexicano*, April 5, 1836.

11 ibid.

12 Susannah Dickinson's testimony is normally used as corroboration that Crockett died at or near the palisade. "I recognized Col. Crockett lying dead and mutilated between the church and the two story barrack building," she said, " – and even remember seeing his peculiar cap lying by his side." (The account appeared in *The History of Texas from Its First Discovery and Settlement* by James M. Morphis, published in 1875.) However, in an account written about her official testimony, there comes a more equivocal statement: "Col. Crockett was one of the 3 men who came into the Fort during the siege and before the assault. He was killed, she believes." (This report is in the State Adjutant General's papers at the Texas State Archives.)

13 Morphis, James M, *The History of Texas from Its First Discovery and Settlement*. New York: United States Publishing Co., 1875, p175.

14 For complete transcriptions of all the survivors' testimonies, see: *The Blood of Noble Men* by Alan Huffines, illustrated by Gary Zaboly, and *Eyewitness to the Alamo* by Bill Groneman. (See the bibliography for full information.)

15 For a thorough look at the issue, see Bill Groneman's *Defense of a Legend: Crockett and the de la Peña Diary* (which asserts that the document is probably a forgery) and James E. Crisp's introduction to the expanded edition of *With Santa Anna in Texas*, Carmen Perry's translation of Peña's work. Crisp believes that the "diary" is probably genuine. (For full details, see the bibliography.)

16 "The Little Book That Wasn't There: The Myth and Mystery of the de la Peña Diary," *Southwestern Historical Quarterly* 98, no. 2 (October 1994), pp261-296.

THE AFTERMATH

Even for such a "small affair" as the battle of the Alamo, the carnage was ghastly. "It was a fearful sight," wrote Sergeant Francisco Becerra of the Matamoros Battalion. "Our lifeless soldiers covered the grounds surrounding the Alamo. They were heaped inside the fortress. Blood and brains covered the earth and floors, and had spattered the walls. The ghostly faces of our comrades met our gaze, and we removed them with despondent hearts."[1]

Eulaia Yorba, a young girl who lived in town, accompanied a priest into the Alamo "to do what we could for the dying men....

The stones in the church wall were spotted with blood, the doors were splintered and battered in. Pools of thick blood were so frequent on the sun-baked earth about the stone building that we had to be careful to avoid stepping in them ... no one could even tell you of the horror of the scene...."[2]

This was the sight that greeted the eyes of the Alamo survivors who, as they were removed from the church, wandered into the terrible landscape in disbelief, numbed by grief, fear and exhaustion. Susannah Dickinson could add physical pain to her litany of woes – she had been shot in the leg,

probably by accident, as she was leaving the church. The women and children who had endured the siege – and had so recently lost their husbands and fathers – were led out of the fort and taken to the local home of Don Ramón Músquiz on what is now South Alamo street. There they were fed meat, bread and coffee. "I recollect that I ate heartily," said Enrique Esparza many years later, "but my mother very sparingly."[3] Later in the afternoon, they were interviewed by Santa Anna, then given a blanket and two silver pesos and released.

FUNERAL PYRES

In and around the Alamo, the rest of the day on March 6 was spent simply in addressing the gory problem of the hundreds of dead bodies. According to Santa Anna's orders, the remains of the Mexican soldiers would be buried and those of the Alamo defenders would be burned. A company of dragoons was sent to gather wood and brush to build funeral pyres on which the corpses would be stacked. The pyres were built in layers – one of wood, one of bodies – then soaked with lantern oil before being set ablaze. One of the pyres was built in the plaza just in front of the church, while two more were built on the *alameda* or what is now Commerce Street. Building the pyres at such a distance from the Alamo was perhaps dictated by the greater availability of wood there, or maybe because of the number of bodies in the vicinity – including the seventy-or-so defenders who may have run in that direction.

"I did not go to the plaza when the dead were burned," recalled a local boy, Juan Díaz, many years later. "I had no desire to see that great funeral pyre, but the odor of it permeated every part of the city. It was sickening and for weeks and months people shunned the Alamo."[4]

Most of the Mexican dead were buried but some reports claimed that their numbers were too numerous, and many corpses were hurled into the San Antonio River. More died in the days following the assault; a dearth of medical care spelled almost certain doom for all who

THE MEN WHO RAN

For those who see the Alamo as a massacre in which every Texan fought bravely to the last, the idea of some of them surviving the battle only to be executed later is bad enough. But the thought that men – perhaps as many as 100 – fled the fort and were killed in the open ground beyond seems almost blasphemy.

But did all the defenders actually die in the Alamo? Probably not. At least one Texian was discovered much later in the day hiding under a bridge. A local woman doing her washing saw him and reported him to some nearby soldiers, who immediately killed him. Then there is the puzzling story of Henry Warnell, who died three months later, in Port Lavacca, on the Gulf Coast of Texas. A sworn statement in an 1858 land claim says that he died of wounds received at the battle of the Alamo. Frustratingly, there are no other details on just how he got out of the fort, and how he made his way to the coast.

There was also Brigido Guerrero, one of the *Tejano* defenders of the Alamo. Confronted by Mexican soldiers during the battle, he somehow convinced them that he had been captured by the Texians and held prisoner in the Alamo. They believed this lucky man and let him go.

But the most shocking incident of the battle, and the one that shakes the Last Stand myth to its very foundations, is the reported flight from the Alamo of two or three groups of men at some point late in the battle. Since none of them actually escaped, it's impossible to know if they were simply running scared or if they had a plan. Either way, it didn't work out well for them. Throughout the battle, lancers patrolled the perimeter of the fort, looking out for just such an action. According to reports, as soon as the Texians got outside the walls, they were quickly cut down. Several Mexican officers reported the incident – Almonte, Peña, Ramírez y Sesma. They all interpreted it as an escape attempt; and there doesn't seem to be any other way to look at it.

Captain Manuel Loranca reported that "sixty-two Texians who sallied from the east side of the fort were received by the lancers and all killed. Only one of these made resistance; a very active man, armed with a double barrel gun and a single barrel pistol, with which he killed a corporal of the lancers named Eugenio. These were all killed by the lance, except one, who ensconced himself under a bush and it was necessary to shoot him."[5]

RIGHT: Death of Dickinson *by Theodore Gentilz. The artist seems to have invented this odd episode out of whole cloth, or misinterpreted some other story which he gathered while researching this and his epic painting* Fall of the Alamo *(1885). Almeron Dickinson did indeed have a daughter who survived the battle, along with Dickinson's wife Susannah. But no known reports of the battle suggest such a scene as Gentilz represents here. [DRT Library, The Alamo.]*

ABOVE: *An idealized (and perhaps apocryphal) portrait of James Walker Fannin, the commander of the Texians at La Bahia in Goliad. An indecisive leader, Fannin tried and failed to come to Travis's aid at the Alamo. He was executed with nearly four hundred of his men on March 27, 1836. This painting has been attributed to Samuel Morse, the inventor of the Morse Code. [Dallas Historical Society.]*

sustained serious wounds during the battle.

But the wounded and dead seemed to mean little to Santa Anna. He referred to them as "chickens" and regarded their sacrifice as a minor but necessary inconvenience. Besides, he still had the rest of Texas to conquer. General Urrea was ordered to attack Colonel (formerly Captain) Fannin's forces at Goliad with his 1,400 men, to be reinforced by a column under Colonel Morales. General Antonio Gaona, with 700 men, was to head toward Nacogdoches by way of Bastrop and Washington-on-the-Brazos. And General Ramírez y Sesma, in command of 1,500 men, marched toward Gonzales and San Felipe de Austin. Santa Anna, for the time being, would remain in his command center at Béxar.

At La Bahía (or "Fort Defiance") in Goliad, Colonel James Walker Fannin had at last decided to act. Keenly aware of his deficiencies as a commander – he had written more than one pleading letter asking to be

relieved of his command – Fannin was also aware of Travis's desperate position at the Alamo. He had, however, never quite been able to go to Travis's assistance. The one time he and his men did start marching toward Béxar, on February 26, lost oxen and broken wagons stopped them in their tracks within 250 yards of Goliad. After a frustrating day and night, Fannin and his officers decided that leaving La Bahía wasn't such a good idea after all. So he returned to the fort and stayed there, "waiting," as historian Stephen L. Hardin has written, "for someone in charge to tell him what to do, waiting for fate to overtake him."[6]

On March 13 or 14, someone in charge did indeed tell Fannin what to do. Houston ordered him to abandon Fort Defiance and to head toward Victoria, urging that "prompt movements are … highly important." But Fannin seemed incapable of doing anything promptly. He lingered for the better part of the week, not managing to prepare for retreat until March 19. Even then, his old problem with oxen and wagons returned to haunt him, making the traveling slower than before; further, a howitzer broke down. After traveling most of the day, Fannin's men had covered barely six miles and were stranded in the open plain.

FANNIN'S FATAL MISTAKE

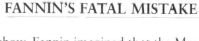

Somehow, Fannin imagined that the Mexicans would not attack a force nearly 400 strong, but he was wrong – and the mistake cost him his life, as well as the lives of nearly every man in his command. The combined troops of Urrea and Morales caught up with Fannin near Coleto Creek. Fannin tried to advance to a slight rise about 500 yards away, believing that it would afford better protection. But when an ammunition wagon broke down, he ordered his men to form a square right there on the spot. The Mexicans lay siege, first killing as many of Fannin's animals as possible, then firing on the men. Fannin himself was wounded in the leg.

Through the night, Fannin's men dug trenches and made fortifications of earth and animal carcasses. But by the next morning they knew that the fight was over. Under a white flag, Fannin surrendered under discretion and he and his men were marched back to La Bahía and imprisoned there for a week. On Sunday, March 27, the Texians were marched from the fort in three groups. Once they were some distance away, the Mexicans stopped them, then opened fire. About twenty-eight Texians escaped in the confusion,

RIGHT: *The execution of Fannin's men in the fields outside Fort Defiance in Goliad, as envisioned by artist Norman Price. [Texas State Library and Archives Commission.]*

FOLLOWING PAGE: *The (now restored) banner of Sidney Sherman's Kentucky volunteers was carried into battle at San Jacinto. [Texas State Library and Archives Commission.]*

running in panic toward the river, but 342 of Fannin's men were killed. Fannin himself, and other wounded Texians who couldn't join in the death march, were executed at La Bahía. It was Palm Sunday.

News of the disasters at the Alamo and Goliad spread across Texas along with the reports that the Mexican army was on the march, destroying everything in its path. Volunteers in the Texian army began to desert and throughout the territory families abandoned their homes to flee for safety in what was called the "Runaway Scrape." At the lowest point of the "Scrape," the Texian army dwindled to just 500 men.

HOUSTON'S TACTICAL RETREAT

On March 31, Santa Anna left San Antonio de Béxar to join Ramírez y Sesma's army. Houston's army, now numbering around 1,000 men, kept moving southeastward in a controversial move that was, according to some, a retreat toward the U.S. border or, according to others, a canny ploy to lull Santa Anna into a false sense of security until the perfect place could be found to attack him. Houston himself later said that he had "determined to retreat and get as near to Andrew Jackson and the old flag as I could."[7] But no matter what was behind the march, the opportunity soon presented itself for Houston to catch Santa Anna by surprise.

The Mexican general, who had just been joined by General Cos's 400 men, camped alongside the bayou at San Jacinto. Santa Anna knew that Houston's army was nearby, and prepared to receive an attack. But when that attack did not come, his exhausted troops virtually collapsed into their *siesta*. It was then, at about 4:30 in the afternoon, that Houston attacked. Before the Mexicans could even mount much of a defense, the Texians were on them shouting, "Remember the Alamo – Remember La Bahía!"

Houston's attack was part battle, part slaughter. All the pent-up anger and anguish the Texians had felt over the devastating recent losses came pouring from them in an orgy of violence. Many Mexicans pleaded for their lives, crying, "Me no Alamo!", but the Texians killed them anyway. The brave General Castrillón was wounded but refused to prostrate himself before the enemy. As he stood calmly facing the Texians, arms folded, he was shot down in cold blood.

Santa Anna did not act as bravely as Castrillón. Asleep in his tent, he was awakened when the attack began, then ran into the woods and hid. He was discovered later in the day, dressed as a common *soldado*, and brought before Sam Houston to work out terms of surrender. The battle of San Jacinto had lasted a mere eighteen minutes. But in that time more than 650 Mexicans were killed by the vengeful army of Sam Houston. Nine Texians were killed and sixty were wounded.

THE MEXICAN RETREAT

San Jacinto has always been seen as the decisive victory that won Texas's independence. But had the Mexicans continued their advance on the colonies, the outcome would not have been nearly so easily predicted. Santa Anna, in order to save his life, relinquished Mexico's claim to Texas and ordered his generals back to Mexico. Intending to merely regroup and attack again later, General Filisola started south with his men. But terrible weather soon bogged them down in what they called the *Mar de Lodo* – the Sea of Mud. They left behind a roadway virtually paved with abandoned ammunition and equipment as they trudged step by painful step toward home, often knee-deep in mud. Once across the Rio Grande, the army was too disheveled and exhausted to mount another march into Texas.

RIGHT: *Sam Houston is said to have had three horses shot out from under him at San Jacinto. The most famous of them was Saracen, a brilliant white steed. The horse shown here is obviously one of Saracen's successors. From the book* Pioneer Heroes and Daring Deeds, *Scammell & Company, 1882. [Craig R. Covner Collection.]*

BELOW: *The capture of Santa Anna is pictured derisively in the book* Pioneer Heroes and Daring Deeds. *The caption reads, "The finding of 'The Mighty and Glorious.'" [Craig R. Covner Collection.]*

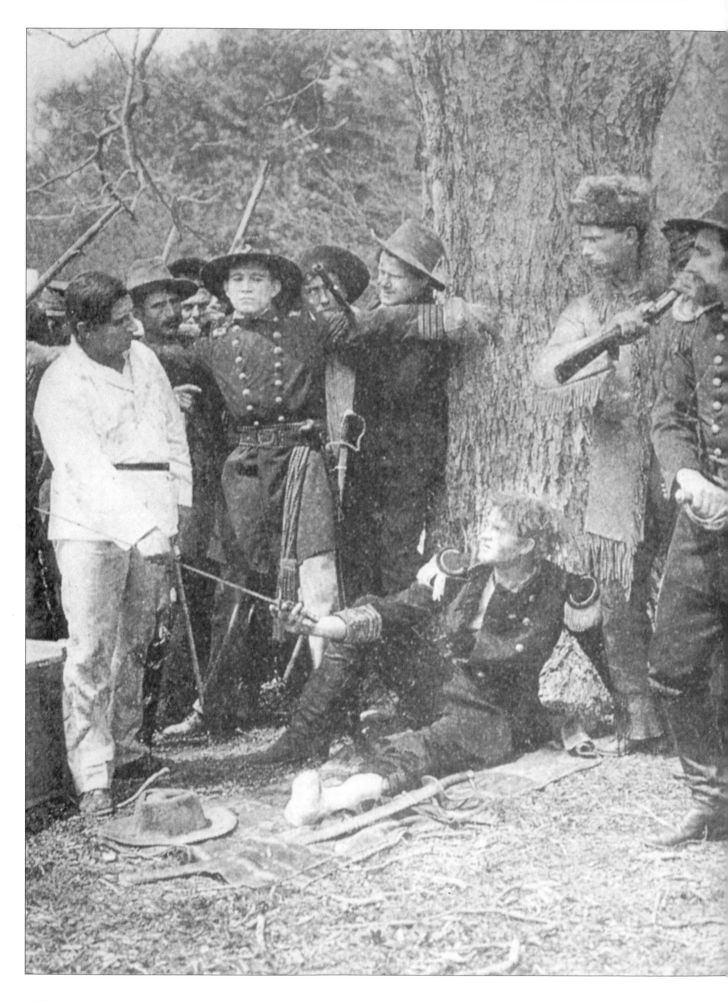

ABOVE: *Joseph Boggs Beale's magic lantern slide "Santa Ana [sic] & Gen. Sam Houston at San Jacinto" ca. 1908. [Jack Judson, The Magic Lantern Castle.]*

LEFT: *Santa Anna's surrender as depicted in the first Alamo movie,* The Immortal Alamo, *filmed in March, 1911, near San Antonio. [Author Collection.]*

The Texas Revolution was over. What had once been a vast Mexican province was now on the road to becoming an independent republic and, a decade later, one of the United States. From the blood shed at the Alamo six weeks earlier had come the independence of which Travis had only dreamed. His defeat had been transformed into victory.

REFERENCES

1   Huffines, Alan, with Zaboly, Gary, *The Blood of Noble Men.* Austin: Eakin Press, 1999, p190.
2   *San Antonio Express*, April 12, 1896.
3   Esparza, Enrique, *San Antonio Express*, May 12 and 19, 1907.
4   Díaz, Juan, *The San Antonio Light*, September 1, 1907.
5   *San Antonio Express*, June 23, 1878.
6   Hardin, Stephen L., *The Alamo 1836: Santa Anna's Texas Campaign.* Oxford: Osprey Publishing, 2001, p60.
7   ibid p73.

THE CHANGING FACE
OF THE ALAMO

The physical site that we now know of as "The Alamo" only barely resembles the mission/fort defended by Bowie, Crockett, Travis and the rest. In fact, the mission compound has been in an almost constant state of flux since construction began in the 1750s.

For nearly a decade after the battle, the Alamo lay in ruins, destroyed not entirely by battle but by design of the Mexican Army, to discourage other rebels from occupying the place. When Santa Anna left with his troops, General Juan Andrade remained behind with about a thousand men to refortify the Alamo. He left no record of what improvements were made over the next two months, but they may have been formidable, given what Green B. Jameson had accomplished in half that time with a quarter the number of men. It was Andrade's task to make sure that the Alamo remained effective as part of Béxar's fortifications. Once Santa Anna won the war, the Alamo would still be what it was under General Cos – the most important military stronghold in the area.

But Santa Anna didn't win the war. After he was defeated by Houston at San Jacinto, orders were sent to Andrade to tear down the Alamo, spike the cannon, toss all the ammunition into the river, and generally render the place uninhabitable and

undefendable. His troops, undoing what they had just spent two months doing, tore down most of the walls and set fire to the church.

This incident inspired an evocative Alamo legend. Adina de Zavala, granddaughter of Lorenzo de Zavala, one of the signatories to the Declaration of Texan Independence, wrote that Andrade's men were met by spirits wielding "flaming swords" and shouting, "Depart, touch not these walls! He who desecrates these walls shall meet a horrible Fate! Multiplied afflictions shall seize upon him and a horrible and agonizing and avenging torture shall be his death!" She continued to say that the angry ghosts "barred [the soldiers'] progress and soon frightened them off; that almost as fast as new relays of men were sent with orders to destroy the

ABOVE: *The first photograph of the Alamo – indeed, the earliest known photo taken in Texas. This 1849 daguerreotype was discovered in the 1990s. It is the only known photo of the church before the "hump" was added by the U.S. Army in about 1850. [Prints and Photograph Collection, The Center For American History, University of Texas – Austin.]*

LEFT: *An 1838 drawing of the ruins of the Alamo by Mary Ann Adams Maverick. [Author Collection.]*

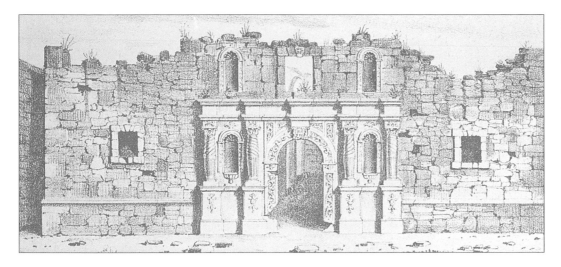

walls, they were overcome by fright; nor could threats or punishment induce them to return. They were permitted by the ghosts for a space to disarm the batteries, but the moment the walls of the buildings were threatened, there was the flaming sword in ghostly hands."[1]

In reality, when Andrade and his men left Béxar on May 24 to join the Mexican army at Goliad, all that was left of the compound was the ruins of the Alamo church, the building that contained the south wall gate and a couple of rooms (later referred to as the *Galera*), and most of the Long Barracks. Along the west wall, a few ruined houses still stood. Soon, some of these were repaired and inhabited once again. Other citizens of Béxar used the Alamo ruins as a kind of free store of building supplies, taking stone and wood from the surviving buildings to use on their own homes.

What little was left of the Alamo was saved by the U. S. Army, beginning in 1847. They had no intention of again using the Alamo as a fort, but decided to remodel the surviving buildings for use as headquarters, with a supply depot, offices, storage facilities, blacksmith shop, and stables.

The Long Barracks was converted into a large versatile building with plenty of space for offices, workshops and living quarters. The south wall gate and its adjoining rooms – the Galera – was also remodeled, using southern pine, shingles and plaster. While clearing out the ruined church, several skeletons and other items were found in the rubble, possible relics of the fall of the Alamo.

A second floor was added to the church and the building was topped with a peaked wooden roof. To disguise the slope of the roof, a humped gable, of Moorish design, was added to the top of the church. Today, this single design element identifies the Alamo more immediately than anything else – but it has nothing to do with the 1836 siege.

In addition to the "hump," the church was otherwise modified and, according to many

103

RIGHT: *This interior view of the Alamo courtyard, in 1911, shows the last scraps of the Long Barracks after the Hugo & Schmeltzer walls have been removed. [Coppini Collection, DRT Library, The Alamo.]*

critics, mutilated. Since its only windows were the two in the front, several more were cut into the thick limestone walls, on all four sides of the building. Two upper windows were added to the façade.

The Alamo remained a U.S. Army depot for almost three decades – except for four years, (1861-1865) – when it served as Confederate Army headquarters. After the Army did abandon the Alamo in 1878, a local merchant, French-born Honore Grenet, bought it and turned the historic ruins into a gaudy, two story shopping center, offering, according to an advertisement of the time, "Groceries, Provisions, Dry Goods, Queensware, Glassware, Boots, Shoes, Whiskeys, Wines, Beers, Cigars, Tobacco, and Country Produce, second to none in the city." When Grenet died in 1882, The Hugo & Schmeltzer Mercantile Company bought the property for $28,000 – but they weren't allowed to lease the church; that was sold in 1883 by the Catholic Church to the state of Texas for $20,000.

It was now up to a small group of patriotic Texans – primarily the new organization The Daughters of the Republic of Texas (DRT) – to reclaim the Long Barracks and present the Alamo "properly" as an historical site. Yet, in the process of doing so, the DRT split into two bitter factions over the matter of interpretation. One side, headed by Adina de Zavala, believed that the Alamo should be restored to some semblance of its original appearance as a mission. She believed that the main historic building on the grounds was the Long Barracks and that the church had played

a relatively minor role in the siege and battle.

On the other side was Clara Driscoll, a wealthy Texan, both of whose grandfathers had fought for the Republic of Texas. Contrary to the view held by de Zavala, Driscoll believed that the church was "The Alamo" and everything else should go. In 1900, she bemoaned the state of "our Alamo … how do we treat it? We leave it hemmed in on one side by a hideous barracks-like looking building, and on the other by two saloons.... Today the Alamo should stand out free and clear. All the unsightly obstructions that hide it away should be torn down and the space utilized for a park. I am sure that if this matter were taken up by some enterprising, patriotic Texan, a sufficient amount could be raised that would enable something of this kind to be done."[2]

In this letter, Driscoll makes clear the fundamental difference between how she viewed the Alamo and how Adina de Zavala viewed it. Driscoll's "hemmed in" Alamo is clearly the church only. The "hideous barracks-like building" – the Hugh & Schmeltzer store – was not historic in itself, but merely a blot that should be removed.

At first, Driscoll and de Zavala were staunch allies. Together, they arranged to purchase the Long Barracks from merchant Charles Hugo – but it was Driscoll who put up the money (eventually, she was reimbursed by the state of Texas) and it was Driscoll's version of the Alamo that has been preserved today. The Hugo & Schmeltzer walls were removed from the Long Barracks and, in 1913, the tattered remains of the barracks' second story

REFERENCES
1   De Zavala, Adina, *History and Legends of the Alamo and other Missions in and Around San Antonio.* San Antonio: by the author, 1917. New edition: Houston: Arte Publico Press, 1996, pp51-52.
2   *San Antonio Express*, April 29, 1900.

was demolished to better emphasize the view of the church.

Clara Driscoll clearly won the "second battle of the Alamo." She is widely remembered today as the "Savior of the Alamo" and is the architect behind what stands there now; it is Clara Driscoll's ideal Alamo that visitors see today. Thanks to her, most people think of the Alamo as a single building with a distinctive gabled façade – not the vast mission compound where so many heroes died in 1836.

LEFT: *A colored woodcut engraving, based on Edward Everett's interior view of the Alamo, painted in 1847. Everett painted several valuable views of the Alamo just prior to its renovation in 1850 by the U.S. Army. [Author Collection.]*

LEFT: *Traveler Phocian R. Way made this sketch in 1858 when the Alamo was headquarters for the Army. New walls have been built over the Long Barracks's stone, and the church has a roof, a new humped gable and several additional windows. [Craig R. Covner Collection.]*

LEFT: *Copy by Craig R. Covner of a watercolor by Seth Eastman depicting the façade of the Alamo church in 1848. [Courtesy of the Artist.]*

LEFT: *This painting by Craig R. Covner, after William Bollaert, shows the Alamo from the southwest in 1843. This view offers a rare look at the south wall gate or* Galera, *which was razed in 1871. [Courtesy of the Artist.]*

THE HEROES OF THE ALAMO,

AND NOW STANDING AT THE ENTRANCE TO THE STATE HOUSE AT AUSTIN, TEXAS.

LEFT: *This Alamo monument was carved in 1841 from actual stones from the Alamo. It stood in Austin at the State Capitol building from 1858 until 1881, when it was destroyed in a fire. [Author Collection.]*

FAR LEFT: *This proposed Alamo monument from 1912 looms over the actual Alamo like a skyscraper. The Shrine can barely be seen at the bottom left of the picture. [DRT Library, The Alamo.]*

RIGHT: *This peculiar Alamo graced the pages of Harper's Weekly on March 23, 1861. It depicts the surrender of U.S. troops to the Confederate Army under General Twigg. The proportions of the building are off, the spiraled columns have been transformed into statues, and the South Wall gate (or Galera) seems to sit beside the church rather than several yards to the southeast. [Author Collection.]*

RIGHT: *An idealized view of the Alamo ruins, first published in Gleason's Pictorial Drawing Room Companion in 1854. It was probably based on Edward Everett's more authentic drawing from 1850. [Author Collection.]*

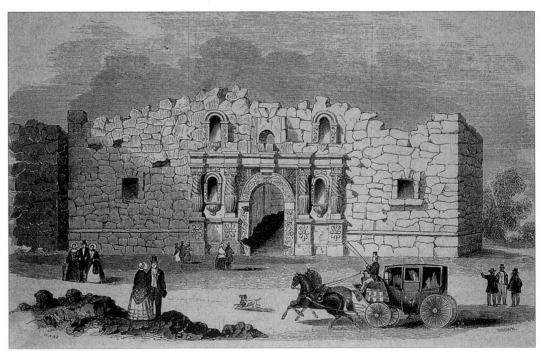

RIGHT: *The Alamo as a shopping mall in about 1880. Store owner Honore Grenet played upon the site's military past by creating an ornate wooden fort over the ruins of the Long Barracks. In one form or another, these walls remained in place until 1911. [Author Collection.]*

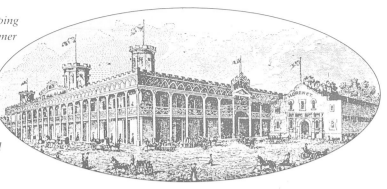

BELOW: *The interior of the Alamo courtyard in 1911 as the Hugo & Schmeltzer walls are being removed. [DRT Library, The Alamo.]*

ABOVE: *Alamo Plaza in about 1906. The church is still acting as a warehouse to the adjacent Hugo & Schmeltzer stores. [Author Collection.]*

RIGHT: *The Alamo in about 1910, still sporting some of the Hugo & Schmeltzer walls. [Coppini Collection, DRT Library, The Alamo.]*

BELOW: *Alamo Plaza ca. 1910. Some of the Hugo & Schmeltzer walls are still standing, though most of the ornate elements have already been removed. [Author Collection.]*

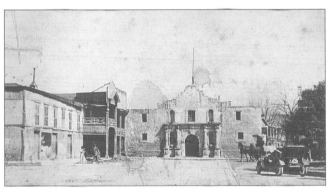

ABOVE: *The fragments of the Long Barracks in 1912. A year later, the top portion will be removed and a back wall built from these and other stones to create what is now the "Long Barracks Museum." [Author Collection.]*

THE ALAMO IN ENTERTAINMENT AND COMMERCE

As Santa Anna's army rode out of San Antonio de Béxar after the battle of the Alamo, the smoking ruin of the old mission/fort stood on the outskirts of town. Today, the Alamo stands at the heart of San Antonio, both literally and figuratively. It is at once the city's most visited site – indeed, in attracting some four million visitors per year, it is one of the most popular historical sites in the United States – and its most revered symbol. Hundreds of businesses and organizations use the word "Alamo" in their names or incorporate part of the church's design, usually the humped gable, into their signs and logos. Some businesses – not only in San Antonio, but in all parts of the United States – have even built replicas of the Alamo to serve as their headquarters in homage to the famous old fort.

The Alamo has clearly become something far more than simply the site of an historical battle. To some, it represents courage, sacrifice, and the cost of liberty. To others, it is an enduring symbol of ethnic bitterness. The Alamo is a shining beacon of patriotic pride, a backdrop for silly movie comedies, a trademark for sports teams, cheerleading schools, plumbing businesses, and restaurants. The Alamo is, in short, virtually a blank slate onto which almost any philosophy can be written.

Even from the beginning, the Alamo was transformed from a place and event in history to an idea. When Sam Houston's men cried "Remember the Alamo" at San Jacinto, the slogan came directly from their hearts, still broken by the loss of so many friends, brothers, and compatriots. But as "Remember the Alamo" spread across the nation, then the world, the concept became more abstract and the Alamo became almost a mythic place on which was played out an eternal struggle of good and evil.

From the beginning, the story of the Alamo was celebrated in poems and songs. The first play on the subject, *The Fall of the Alamo or Texas and the Oppressors* (author unknown), premiered in Philadelphia in May, 1836 – less than three months after the battle. It was followed by many more theatrical presentations, the most recent of which (at this writing) is *Liberty! The Siege of the Alamo*, a musical drama that premiered in 1999.

When the medium of the motion picture was born around the turn of the 20th Century, the exciting saga of the Alamo began to be committed to celluloid. The first Alamo film was *The Immortal Alamo*, released on May 25, 1911. It was filmed in San Antonio, not far from the site of the actual battle. This one-reel silent film was followed by many more

RIGHT: *The image of the Alamo has even been used to sell cars. This is Alamo Auto Auctions in San Antonio, Texas. [Photograph by Joan Headley.]*

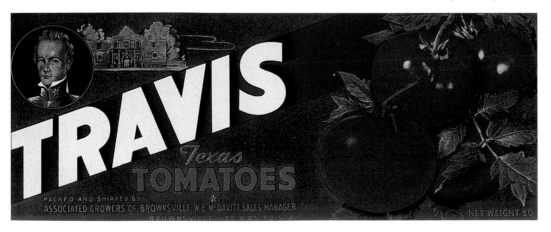

LEFT: *Texas tomato growers used the image of both the Alamo and its young commander in this colorful label from the 1930s. By this point, the Alamo was being used in ways that had little or no connection to the battle fought there in 1836. [Author Collection.]*

cinematic treatments of the story including *The Martyrs of the Alamo* (1915), *Heroes of the Alamo* (1937), *The Last Command* (1955), and John Wayne's epic *The Alamo* (1960).

When Walt Disney's three-part television series on Davy Crockett premiered on the program *Disneyland* late in 1954, it began a fad among the world's young people that would be superceded only by Beatlemania a decade later. Suddenly, the Alamo was more than simply an event in a history book – it was the subject of wholesome fun. Its image adorned bed sheets, pajamas, bicycle seats, costumes, pinball games, camping tents, comic books, trading cards, coloring books, records and countless other items. With "The Official Walt Disney's Davy Crockett at the Alamo" playset, a young Crockett buff could fight the entire battle again and again with plastic soldiers inside a lithographed metal fort.

Pretty girls, pretty girls everywhere, But the SAN ANTONIO BELLES are claimed most fair.

San Antonio, Tex. The Alamo –

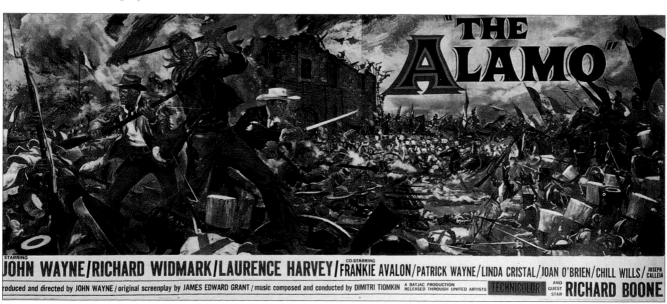

"THE ALAMO"

STARRING
JOHN WAYNE/RICHARD WIDMARK/LAURENCE HARVEY/ CO-STARRING FRANKIE AVALON/PATRICK WAYNE/LINDA CRISTAL/JOAN O'BRIEN/CHILL WILLS/ JOSEPH CALLEIA

roduced and directed by JOHN WAYNE / original screenplay by JAMES EDWARD GRANT / music composed and conducted by DIMITRI TIOMKIN A BATJAC PRODUCTION RELEASED THROUGH UNITED ARTISTS TECHNICOLOR AND GUEST STAR RICHARD BOONE

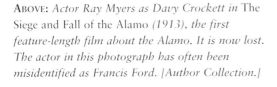

ABOVE: *Actor Ray Myers as Davy Crockett in* The Siege and Fall of the Alamo *(1913), the first feature-length film about the Alamo. It is now lost. The actor in this photograph has often been misidentified as Francis Ford. [Author Collection.]*

RIGHT, TOP: *A painted backdrop serves as the Alamo in the first film on the subject,* The Immortal Alamo, *filmed in San Antonio in March 1911. [Author Collection.]*

RIGHT, MIDDLE: *The set built for the 1915 production of* The Martyrs of the Alamo *or* The Birth of Texas, *a film supervised (produced) by the legendary American filmmaker D. W. Griffith. [Author Collection.]*

RIGHT: *Alamo set constructed for Ramsey Yelvington's play* A Cloud of Witnesses. *[Author Collection.]*

LEFT: *An unusually authentic Alamo replica constructed for the Errol Flynn Western San Antonio (1945). As usual, the filmmakers mix fact with fancy: the Alamo church is equipped with its humped gable, but the inside is still roofless and filled with debris. Paul Kelly is the menacing villain at the door. He will soon join the ranks of those killed in the Alamo. [Warner Bros.]*

BELOW: *A fairly convincing reproduction of San Antonio – and a strikingly authentic Alamo replica – from the Errol Flynn western San Antonio (1945). [Warner Bros., Paul A. Hutton Collection.]*

TODAY AND TOMORROW **ROYAL THEATER** **TODAY AND TOMORROW**

THE SEASON'S GREATEST SUCCESS

THE SIEGE AND FALL OF THE ALAMO

IN MOTION PICTURES—MADE IN SAN ANTONIO

AT A COST OF MORE THAN $35,000.00

A Correct Reproduction of the Most Tragic Event in Texas History

5 GREAT REELS—Perfect acting—superb photography—cast of 2000 will be shown again today and tomorrow—*Be sure and see it—send the children.*

ADMISSION 10c AND 20c

ABOVE: *An advertisement for the first feature-length Alamo movie – now lost. [Author Collection.]*

BELOW: *Advertisement for* The Immortal Alamo *(1911). [Author Collection.]*

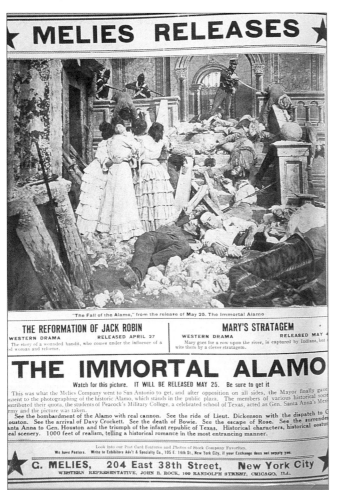

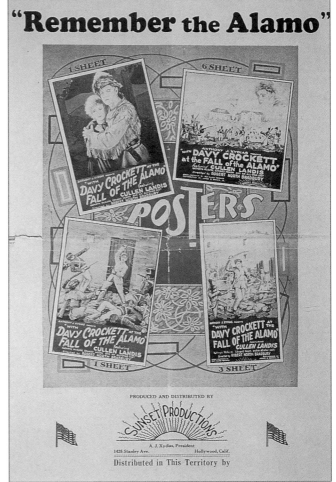

ABOVE: *An assortment of posters advertising the low-budget silent epic* With Davy Crockett at the Fall of the Alamo *(1926) starring Cullen Landis as Crockett. [Author Collection.]*

RIGHT: A flyer advertising Ramsey Yelvington's Alamo play A Cloud of Witnesses. Because the title didn't seem descriptive enough, the words "Drama of the Alamo" are given greater prominence. [Author Collection.]

LEFT: *The Alamo church as recreated for John Wayne's* The Alamo *(1960). The anachronistic upper windows are there and art director Al Ybarra was instructed by Wayne to give the ruined top a bit of a curve, to suggest the hump. The cross was placed there after Wayne ordered Ybarra to "Give me something allegorical." [Author Collection.]*

LEFT: *Conceptual painting by John Jensen for John Wayne's film* The Alamo *(1960). [John Jensen; Dan Gagliasso Collection.]*

FAR RIGHT: *Davy Crockett (John Wayne) in* The Alamo *(1960) wields the same steel-bladed prop Bowie knife created for the 1952 Warner Bros. film* The Iron Mistress. *[United Artists; Joseph Musso Collection.]*

RIGHT: *John Wayne produced a behind-the-scenes special,* The Spirit of the Alamo, *which aired on NBC Television in conjunction with the release of* The Alamo. *[Author Collection.]*

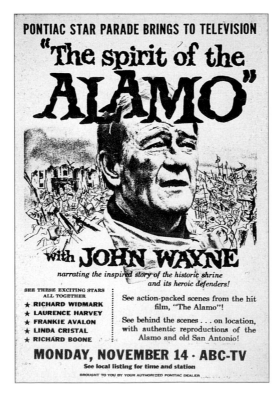

ABOVE LEFT: *Alan Ladd as Jim Bowie, overshadowed by the knife that bears his name. From the film* The Iron Mistress *(1953). [Warner Bros; Author Collection.].*

ABOVE: *The Alamo's "Holy Trinity" – as seen on television: (l. to r.) Grant Show as Travis, John Schneider as Crockett, and David Keith as Bowie. From the mini-series* James A. Mitchener's Texas. *[Republic Pictures; Author Collection.]*

LEFT: *Fess Parker (center) as Davy Crockett, holding the very rifle described on page 61. To his left is Buddy Ebsen as Georgie Russel. From* Davy Crockett, King of the Wild Frontier *(1955). [Walt Disney Productions; Joseph Musso Collection.]*

BELOW: *The Alamo set at Happy Shahan's Alamo Village, ca. 1987. Originally built for John Wayne's* The Alamo *in 1959, the set had recently been refurbished for the IMAX production* Alamo... the Price of Freedom *(1988). [Photograph by Author.]*

LEFT: *An Alamo pinball game from the 1930s. [Author Collection.]*

BELOW: *The Louis Marx Company's "Official Walt Disney's Davy Crockett at the Alamo" playset, released in 1955. This lithographed metal fort was defended and attacked by 54mm plastic soldiers. [Author Collection.]*

LEFT: *The Alamo playset released by Ideal Toys in the mid-1950s. Molded in bright red plastic, the model only barely resembles the Alamo, but children didn't seem to mind. Nor do current toy collectors. [Author Collection.]*

LEFT: *Metal Alamo toy designed by Craig R. Covner and distributed by Classic Toy Soldiers.* [Author Collection.]

BELOW: *A jigsaw puzzle released in 1955 at the height of the "Crockett Craze." Normally, in popular culture, Crockett's last moments are depicted with the buckskin hero swinging his empty rifle like a club. Here, he dukes it out,* mano a mano, *with his fists.* [Author Collection.]

117

THE ALAMO
AS A MUSEUM

Today, the Alamo continues to be merchandised in almost every manner imaginable. A visit to the museum/gift shop on the Alamo grounds reveals everything from Alamo Christmas ornaments to Alamo pencils and erasers; the list of merchandise literally spans the sublime to the ridiculous.

However, the sale of these items by the museum/gift shop does provide funding that goes toward a worthy cause – the Alamo itself. Since 1905, The Daughters of the Republic of Texas have managed the site without, they proudly claim, a penny from the State of Texas. This enthusiastic and patriotic organization has come under criticism by some scholars and other groups for its rather conservative and unabashedly heroic view of the Battle of the Alamo but they have been faithful to their trust of taking care of Texas's most precious historical site.

A visitor to the Alamo today may at first be surprised to find that it sits squarely in the

BELOW: *Today the site of the Alamo attracts some four million visitors annually. [Craig R. Covner Collection.]*

middle of San Antonio, surrounded by the noise and traffic and tourists and city life. And that visitor might also have a difficult time, at first, reconciling this limestone building with all the epic stories of battle that he has gleaned from movies and other popular culture influences. But there is no mistaking the spirit in which the visitor is expected to tour the site. On the door, a bronze plaque cautions:

> *Be silent, friend*
> *Here heroes died*
> *To pave the way*
> *For other men*

The Alamo is often called "The Shrine of Texas Liberty" and that is precisely how the DRT treat it. Gentlemen are asked to remove their hats and, except on March 6, the anniversary of the battle, there is no photography allowed inside the church – flash or otherwise. A walk through the shrine is not particularly instructive, though there are regular lecture tours and artifacts on display.

But it can be a deeply moving, even inspiring, experience. The hushed atmosphere inside the cool, limestone walls make it *feel* like the shrine that the DRT insists it is, a place for reflection and, perhaps, of prayer.

Outside, one path leads to the museum/gift shop that is, admittedly, far more gift shop than museum. But there are a few more artifacts on view and a large, dramatic diorama, by sculptor Tom Feeley, depicting the battle of the Alamo with thousands of model soldiers and a meticulously recreated Alamo compound.

Just outside the museum/gift shop is the most satisfyingly educational feature on the grounds, the Wall of History. On this long, informative mural is the entire story of the Alamo from mission days through the present. It is heavily illustrated and simply, yet thoroughly, documented. The Alamo visitor who is seriously interested in the history of the site will find the Wall of History to be the perfect introduction and overview.

The Long Barracks Museum, built in the

INTERIOR ALAMO
SAN ANTONIO, TEXAS.

SAN ANTONIO, TEXAS. INTERIOR OF THE ALAMO.

LEFT: *An interior view of one of the Alamo buildings in about 1910, five years after the site, and the legend, came under the stewardship of the Daughters of the Republic of Texas. [Author Collection.]*

BELOW LEFT: *Another interior view of the Alamo as it was in about 1910. Located on Alamo Plaza in downtown San Antonio, the Alamo's three buildings – the Shrine, Long Barracks Museum, and Gift Shop/Museum – house exhibits on the Texas Revolution and Texas history. [Author Collection.]*

ABOVE, RIGHT: *Alamo Plaza, ca. 1912. The fragments of the Long Barracks are still standing. A year later, the top portion will be removed to better enhance the view of the church, the building that is already considered to be "The Alamo." [Author Collection.]*

RIGHT: *The IMAX short film production* Alamo... the Price of Freedom *(1988) was produced on the set originally built for John Wayne's* The Alamo *in 1959. As of this writing, it is still shown daily in San Antonio, in an IMAX theater just behind the Alamo. [Rivertheater Associates.]*

reconstructed ruins of the only other partially surviving building from the mission period, also offers visitors a view of paintings, weapons, and other artifacts, as well as a short video about the Alamo. But just across the street behind the Alamo, in the Rivercenter Mall, is a more entertaining cinematic introduction to the Alamo – the IMAX production *Alamo ... the Price of Freedom*. It was filmed in the summer of 1987 on the same set near Brackettville, Texas, where John Wayne made *The Alamo* in 1959. The huge IMAX images – the screen is 61 x 84 feet –

and the thundering, surround-sound track do serve to place the viewer right in the middle of the battle. But, at just forty minutes, even with all its pomp and ear-splitting cannon blasts, *Alamo ... the Price of Freedom* can offer only a brief – and quite traditional – overview of the events that took place almost 170 years ago.

But then, it seems that no single book, film, poem, or song can ever truly encompass the full epic of the Alamo. For such a "small affair," it still seems too big to grasp, even after so many years and so much research. Perhaps that is what has kept it alive in the imagination of the world for nearly 170 years; it seems so simple and yet remains somehow outside the grasp. And perhaps that is why scholars, historians and other obsessives keep digging into the subject, mining for any additional nugget, no matter how microscopic. For them, it is a quest that has no ending, a story that always changes in the retelling. But they keep plowing away because they want to *know*. They want *answers*.

For the rest of the world, it's enough simply to remember.

121

THE ALAMO DEFENDERS

The following list of the men who made up the Alamo garrison is certainly incomplete and probably contains more than one erroneous name. Research continues to add and subtract from the total. History has generally accepted figures anywhere from one hundred eighty-two to one hundred eighty-nine Alamo defenders, but today we suspect that number to be quite low. Historian Thomas Ricks Lindley of Texas, who has done more research in this area than anyone else, estimates that the list of names will one day climb to well over two hundred and fifty and that several names currently carved in marble on the Alamo Cenotaph are there incorrectly.

Consider this, then, merely a list of most of the men who are believed to have died in the Alamo and let's leave the door open to further revision as time goes on.

Abamillo, Juan – Texas
Allen, Robert – Virginia
Andross, Miles De Forest – Vermont
Autry, Micajah – North Carolina
Badillo, Juan Antonio – Texas
Bailey, Peter James III – Kentucky
Baker, Isaac G. – Arkansas
Baker, William Charles M. – Missouri
Ballentine, Richard W. – Scotland
Ballentine, John J. – Pennsylvania
Baugh, John J. – Virginia
Bayliss, Joseph – Tennessee
Blair, John – Tennessee
Blair, Samuel – Tennessee
Blazeby, William – England
Bonham, James Butler – South Carolina
Bourne, Daniel – England
Bowie, James – Kentucky
Bowman, Jesse B. – Tennessee
Brown, George – England
Brown, James – Pennsylvania
Buchanan, James – Alabama
Burns, Samuel E. – Ireland
Butler, George, D. – Missouri
Cain, John – Pennsylvania
Campbell, Robert – Tennessee
Carey, William R. – Virginia
Clark, Charles Henry – Missouri
Clark, M. B. – Mississippi
Cloud, Daniel William – Kentucky
Cochran, Robert E. – New Hampshire
Cottle, George Washington – Missouri
Courtman, Henry – Germany
Crawford, Lemuel – South Carolina
Crockett, David – Tennessee
Crossman, Robert – Pennsylvania
Cummings, David P. – Pennsylvania
Cunningham, Robert – New York
Darst, Jacob C. – Kentucky
Davis, John – Kentucky

Day, Freeman H.K. – Scotland
Day, Jerry C. – Missouri
Daymon, Squire – Tennessee
Dearduff, William – Tennessee
Dennison, Stephen – England or Ireland
Despallier, Charles – Louisiana
Dewall, Lewis – New York
Dickinson, Almeron – Tennessee
Dillard, John Henry – Tennessee
Dimpkins, James R. – England
Duvalt, Andrew – Ireland
Espalier, Carlos – Texas
Esparza, Gregorio – Texas
Evans, Robert – Ireland
Evans, Samuel B. – New York
Ewing, James L. – Tennessee
Faunterloy, William Keener – Kentucky
Fishbaugh, William – Alabama (?)
Flanders, John – New Hampshire
Floyd, Dolphin Ward – North Carolina
Forsyth, John Hubbard – New York
Fuentes, Antonio – Texas
Fuqua, Galba – Alabama
Garnett, William – Virginia
Garrand, James W. – Louisiana
Garrett, James Girard – Tennessee
Garvin, John E. – Missouri (?)
Gaston, John E. – Kentucky
George, James – Tennessee (?)
Goodrich, John C. – Virginia
Grimes, Albert Calvin – Georgia
Guerrero, José María – Texas
Gwynne, James C. – England
Hannum, James – Pennsylvania
Harris, John – Kentucky
Harrison, Andrew Jackson – Tennessee
Harrison, William B. – Ohio
Hawkins, Joseph M. – Ireland
Hays, John M. – Tennessee
Heiskell, Charles M. – Tennessee

Herndon, Patrick Henry – Virginia
Hersee, William Daniel – England
Holland, Tapley – Ohio
Holloway, Samuel – Pennsylvania
Howell, William D. – Massachusetts
Jackson, Thomas – Ireland
Jackson, William Daniel – Kentucky
Jameson, Green B. – Kentucky
Jennings, Gordon C. – Pennsylvania
Jimenes (Ximenes), Damacio – Texas
Johnson, Lewis – Wales
Johnson, William – Pennsylvania
Jones, John – New York
Kenney, James – Virginia
Kent, Andrew – Kentucky
Kerr, Joseph – Louisiana
Kimbell, George C. – Pennsylvania
King, William Philip – Texas
Lewis, William Irvine – Virginia
Lightfoot, William J. – Virginia
Lindley, Jonathan L. – Illinois
Linn, William – Massachusetts
Losoya, Toribio – Texas
Main, George Washington – Virginia
Malone, William T. – Georgia
Marshall, William – Tennessee
Martin, Albert – Rhode Island
McCafferty, Edward – unknown
McCoy, Jesse – Tennessee
McDowell, William – Pennsylvania
McGee, James – Ireland
McGregor, John – Scotland
McKinney, Robert – Tennessee
Melton, Eliel – Georgia
Miller, Thomas R. – Tennessee
Mills, William – Tennessee
Millsaps, Isaac – Mississippi
Mitchasson, Edward – Virginia
Mitchell, Edwin T. – Georgia
Mitchell, Napoleon B. unknown
Moore, Robert B. – Virginia
Moore, Willis A. – Mississippi
Musselman, Robert – Ohio
Nava, Andrés – Texas
Neggan, George – South Carolina
Nelson, Andrew M. – Tennessee
Nelson, Edward – South Carolina
Nelson, George – South Carolina
Northcross, James – Virginia
Nowlan, James – England
Pagan, George – Mississippi (?)
Parker, Christopher Adam – Mississippi (?)
Parks, William – North Carolina
Perry, Richardson – Texas

Pollard, Amos – Massachusetts
Reynolds, John Purdy – Pennsylvania
Roberts, Thomas H. – England (?)
Robertson, James Waters – Tennessee
Robinson, Isaac – Scotland
Rose, James M. – Ohio
Rusk, Jackson J. – Ireland
Rutherford, Joseph – Kentucky
Ryan, Isaac – Louisiana
Scurlock, Mial – North Carolina
Sewell, Marcus L. – England
Shied, Manson – Georgia
Simmons, Cleveland Kinlock – South
    Carolina
Smith, Andrew H. – Tennessee
Smith, Charles S. – Maryland
Smith, Joshua G. – North Carolina
Smith, William H. – England (?)
Starr, Richard – England
Stewart, James E. – England
Stockton, Richard L. – New Jersey
Summerlin, A. Spain – Tennessee
Summers, William E. – Tennessee
Sutherland, William DePriest – Alabama
Taylor, Edward – Tennessee
Taylor, George – Tennessee
Taylor, James – Tennessee
Taylor, William – Tennessee
Thomas, B. Archer M. – Kentucky
Thomas, Henry – Germany
Thompson, Jesse G. – Arkansas
Thomson, John W. – North Carolina
Thruston, John, M. – Pennsylvania
Trammel, Burke – Ireland
Travis, William Barret – South Carolina
Tumlinson, George W. – Missouri
Tylee, James – New York
Walker, Asa – Tennessee
Walker, Jacob – Tennessee
Ward, William B. – Ireland
Warnell, Henry – Arkansas (?)
Washington, Joseph G. – Kentucky
Waters, Thomas – England
Wells, William – Georgia
White, Isaac – Alabama (?) or Kentucky (?)
White, Robert – England
Williamson, Hiram James – Pennsylvania
Wills, William – Tennessee (?)
Wilson, David L. – Scotland
Wilson, John – Pennsylvania
Wolf, Anthony – England (?)
Wright, Claiborne – North Carolina
Zanco, Charles – Denmark
_____, John, a Black Freedman – unknown

THE ALAMO NONCOMBATANTS AND SURVIVORS

Thermopolae had its messenger of defeat. The Alamo had none! In the legend of the Alamo, every man died at his post and there was no one left to tell the tale. Actually, that isn't quite true. There were several women and children in the fort, families of Alamo defenders. But there were also some who fought at the Alamo and got out alive. In the following list, you will find the names and birthplaces of these survivors as well as a brief identifying note.

Allen, James L. – Kentucky. Courier. Left the Alamo on March 5.

Alsbury, Juana Navarro de – Texas. Wife of Texian scout Dr. Horace Alsbury.

Baylor, John Walker Jr. – Kentucky. Courier. Died at San Jacinto.

Brown, Robert – Texas. Courier. Left the Alamo on February 25.

Castro, Maria de Jesus (Esparza) – Texas. Stepdaughter of Alamo defender Gregorio Esparza.

Cruz y Arocha, Antonio – Texas. Left the Alamo with Juan Seguín on February 25.

De la Garza, Alexandro – Texas. Courier.

Desauque, Francis L. – Pennsylvania. Courier. Died with Fannin at Goliad.

Dickinson, Angelina Elizabeth – Texas. Fifteen-month-old daughter of Alamo defender Almeron Dickinson and Alamo survivor Susannah Dickinson.

Dickinson, Susannah Arabella – Tennessee. Wife of Alamo defender Almeron Dickinson and mother of Alamo survivor Angelina Dickinson.

Dimitt, Philip – Kentucky. Courier. Left the Alamo on February 25.

Esparza, Ana Salazar – Texas. Wife of Alamo defender Gregorio Esparza.

Esparza, Enrique – Texas. Son of Ana and Gregorio Esparza.

Esparza, Francisco – Texas. Son of Ana and Gregorio Esparza.

Esparza, Manuel – Texas. Son of Ana and Gregorio Esparza.

Gonzales, Petra – birthplace unknown. Possible relative of Ana Esparza.

Guerrero, Brigido – Mexico. Tejano defender who was spared when he convinced Mexican soldiers that he had been held prisoner by the Texians.

Highsmith, Benjamin Franklin – Missouri. Courier. Left the Alamo on February 18.

Joe – Alabama. William Barret Travis's Negro slave. Spared by the Mexicans.

Johnson, William P. – birthplace unknown. Courier. His presence at the Alamo is unconfirmed. A man by this name was executed with Fannin at Goliad.

Lockhart, Byrd – Virginia or Mississippi. Left the Alamo with Andrew Sowell (below) to get supplies for the garrison. Never returned.

Losoya, Concepción – Texas. Possibly the mother of Alamo defender Toribio Losoya.

Losoya, Juan – Texas. Possibly the brother of Alamo defender Toribio Losoya.

Melton, Juana – Texas. Wife of Alamo defender Eliel Melton and sister of defender Toribio Losoya.

Navarro, Gertrudis – Texas. Sister of Juana Navarro de Alsbury.

Perez, Alejo Jr. – Texas. Son of Juana Navarro de Alsbury.

Oury, William Sanders – Virginia. Courier. Left the Alamo on February 29.

Patton, William Hester – Kentucky. Courier. Left the Alamo after February 5.

Rose, Louis "Moses" – France. His presence in the Alamo may be a myth. He is said to have left after Travis drew his fabled "line in the sand" on about March 5.

Saucedo, Trinidad – Texas. Former servant to the Veramendi family.

Seguín, Juan Nepomuceno – Texas. Courier. Left the Alamo on February 25.

Smith, John William – Virginia. Courier. Left the Alamo on February 23. Returned with reinforcements from Goliad on March 1 then went out again on March 3.

Smither, Launcelot – birthplace unknown. Courier. Left the Alamo on February 23.

Sowell, Andrew Jackson – Tennessee. Left the Alamo with Byrd Lockhart (above) to get supplies for the garrison. Never returned.

Sutherland, John – Virginia. Claimed to have been an Alamo courier. New evidence suggests that he may have played no part in the siege at all.

Victoriana, Mrs. – birthplace unknown. No information available. Enrique Esparza mentioned seeing her in the Alamo with her daughters.

Wolf Brothers – birthplace unknown. The two sons of Alamo defender Anthony Wolf. Their first names are unknown. Both boys were killed in the battle.

Black slave woman – name unknown. Travis's slave Joe reported seeing her body after the battle.

BIBLIOGRAPHY

Chemerka, William R., *Alamo Almanac & Book of Lists* (1997, Austin: Eakin Press).

Daughters of the Republic of Texas, The, *The Wall of History: The History of the Alamo* (ca. 2001, San Antonio: The Daughters of the Republic of Texas).

Davis, William C., *Three Roads to the Alamo* (1998, New York: Harper Collins).

Dobie, J. Frank, Boatright, Mody C. and Ransom, Harry H., eds., *In the Shadow of History* (1939, Dallas: Texas Folklore Society).

Edmondson, J. R., *The Alamo Story: From Early History to Recent Conflicts* (2000, Plano: Republic of Texas Press).

Groneman, Bill, *Defense of a Legend: Crockett and the de la Peña Diary* (1994, Plano: Republic of Texas Press).

Groneman, Bill, *Eyewitness to the Alamo* (1996, Plano: Republic of Texas Press).

Hardin, Stephen L., *Texian Iliad: A Military History of the Texas Revolution, 1835-1836* (1994, Austin: University of Texas Press).

Hardin, Stephen L., *The Alamo 1836: Santa Anna's Texas Campaign* (2001, Oxford: Osprey Publishing).

Hatch, Thom, *Encyclopedia of the Alamo and the Texas Revolution* (1999, Jefferson, North Carolina: McFarland & Co. Inc.).

Huffines, Alan C., *Blood of Noble Men: The Alamo Siege and Battle – An Illustrated Chronology* (illustrated by Gary S. Zaboly) (1999, Austin: Eakin Press).

Jackson, Jack, *Los Tejanos* (1982, Stamford, CT: Fantagraphics Books, Inc.).

Kilgore, Dan, *How Did Davy Die?* (1978, College Station: Texas A&M Press).

Long, Jeff, *Duel of Eagles* (1990, New York: William Morrow & Co.).

Lord, Walter, *A Time to Stand* (1961, New York: Harper & Brothers).

Matovina, Timothy M., *The Alamo Remembered: Tejano Accounts and Perspectives* (1995, Austin: University of Texas Press).

Myers, John Myers, *The Alamo* (1948, New York: E. P. Dutton & Co.).

Nelson, George, *The Alamo: An Illustrated History* (1998, Dry Frio Canyon, Texas: Aldine Press).

Peña, José Enrique de la (Translated and edited by Carmen Perry, introduction by James E. Crisp), *With Santa Anna in Texas: A Personal Narrative of the Revolution* (Expanded Edition, 1997, College Station: Texas A&M Press).

Rosenthal, Phil and Groneman, Bill, *Roll Call at the Alamo* (1985, Ft. Collins, CO: The Old Army Press).

Schoelwer, Susan Prendergast, and Glaser, Tom W. (introduction by Paul Andrew Hutton), *Alamo Images: Changing Perceptions of a Texas Experience* (1985, Dallas: DeGolyer Library and Southern Methodist University Press).

Thompson, Frank, *Alamo Movies* (1991, East Berlin, Pennsylvania: Old Mill Books).

Thompson, Frank, *The Alamo: A Cultural History* (2001, Dallas: Taylor Publishing Co.).

Tinkle, Lon, *Thirteen Days to Glory: The Siege of the Alamo* (1958, New York: McGraw-Hill Book Co.).

Todish, Tim J., and Todish, Terry S., *Alamo Sourcebook 1836* (1998, Austin: Eakin Press).

Warren, Robert Penn, *Remember the Alamo!* (1958, New York: Random House, Inc.).

INDEX

Figures in **bold** type represent references in captions to illustrations.

`- 6`